# Conflict Resolution for Musicians
# (and Other Cool People)

Conflict Resolution for Musicians (and Other Cool People)
by Helene Arts and Ken Ashdown

© 2015 Helene Arts and Ken Ashdown.

Published by Conflict Resolution for Creatives (CRFC) Press
4955 Somerville Street
Vancouver, BC, Canada
V5W 3H1
1-844-584-4687
crfc@fifthhousegroup.com

For bulk discounts or to reach the authors for speaking engagements, training sessions, or consultation, please contact the publisher or visit the Fifth House Group web site at www..fifthhousegroup.com/crfcpress.html.

ISBN (paperback): 978-0-9940810-0-1

First edition.

Published February, 2015. Printed in the United States.

10 9 8 7 6 5 4 3 2 1

Cover design by Chris Fink-Jensen.

Book design and production by Tod McCoy at Hydra House.

Copy Editor: Jennifer D Munro.

Author photographs by Gordan Dumka (KA) & Jamieson Wolf (HA).

## Dedications

*Helene*: To Emme, Ciaran, and Aisling—the loves of my life. And to the memory of Graham Winston Hancock.

*Ken*: To my parents, with love and gratitude for their lifetime of support, especially during all my years in the music business. And to all musicians everywhere: "Play on; give me excess of it."

# Table of Contents

# Introduction

If you're reading this book, then chances are you're either a musician involved in a conflict or you know one who is. Perhaps conflict is already impacting the group, you're concerned about how to resolve immediate problems, and you want to skip straight to the practical bits to help you deal with pressing issues. That's fine: —*go directly to the section you think will be most helpful right now* (probably Part III: Essential Conflict Prevention and Resolution Skills, starting on page 90). There's no time to waste!

Make sure you come back and read the other sections, though, because they provide valuable context and insight into how conflicts get started in the first place and how they escalate. You will also learn other important aspects of conflict theory, which will help you prevent and deal with conflicts more effectively over the long term.

It may comfort you to know that you're far from alone. The reasons we wrote this book for you were close to home, in a manner of speaking. Over the course of Ken's twenty-year career in the music business, he has seen a disturbingly large number of artists struggle with conflict and ultimately implode, while Helene has worked with hundreds of individuals and teams whose families and workplaces suffered because of conflict. Together we saw far too many individual musicians, duos, groups, and even entire orchestras suffer from internal discord; the world was thus deprived of great music, and it was time to do what we could to prevent such losses to the world.

# A brief history of conflict in music

Lennon and McCartney; Jagger and Richards; Noel and Liam Gallagher; Ray and Dave Davies.... All are world-renowned musicians with massive hit records. Most have also been enormously successful songwriting partnerships. Two of the pairs are siblings. What they all have in common, however—other than substantial critical and financial success in popular music, of course—is that *all of them have suffered from conflict at various points in their careers.*

The conflicts sometimes resulted in disaster, including breakups of the very groups that had made them household names. The conflict at times escalated to physical violence (on or off stage, sometimes both) and led to lengthy, ugly public feuds played out in the news media. While some musicians on this impressive list have gone on to achieve post-group success as solo artists, many have had their careers severely limited or cut short by a premature breakup, often just as their group was reaching its creative or commercial peak. So it goes with many other recording and touring artists: in situations where the conflict is particularly destructive and creates lasting resentment, there may be no hope of a reunion tour or future recordings. Everyone loses, including the fans. A partial list of top artists that have broken up in recent years (with varying degrees of acrimony) includes Smashing Pumpkins, Scissor Sisters, The White Stripes, My Chemical Romance, Sum 41, Fall Out Boy, Paramore, and the Jonas Brothers, to name just a few.

Of course, feuds and rivalries in the music industry did not start in modern times. Although there is some doubt that Wolfgang Amadeus Mozart's alleged conflict with fellow composer/conductor Antonio Salieri was as bitter or as long-running as depicted in the film *Amadeus,* and while it's hard to say how much (if any) financial hardship was caused to either party as a result, it did stoke controversy in social circles that lingers today. And it's well documented that W.S. Gilbert and Arthur Sullivan never matched the success of their earlier collaborative works, such as *H.M.S. Pinafore, The Mikado,* or *The Pirates of*

*Penzance*, after their split and subsequent—if brief—creative reunion. Theirs was a working relationship that had long been filled with tension, so it might have come as no surprise to observers when Gilbert and Sullivan first went their separate ways, or when they eventually parted for good.

Conflicts and their resulting breakups are all the more frustrating for musicians and audiences alike because they're not always easy to predict. They're hard to see coming because no single pattern fits every case. For some groups, having one individual (whether the lead singer, songwriter, or instrumentalist) as a front person is a blessing, while for others it can be a curse. In some groups where all members write or contribute musical ideas, the democratic approach is precisely the thing that most often leads to conflict, while in other groups the opposite may be true. There are issues of control, financial compensation, choice of manager, ownership of band name, the desire to tour or not, and even the order in which artists' names are billed on the marquee. There are as many reasons for conflict as there are bands themselves.

In fact many—perhaps most—causes of internal group conflicts are hidden or incorrectly diagnosed. "Creative differences" is perhaps the most commonly cited cause of group discord, but it's a nebulous, catch-all term that may mask a wide range of underlying problems. Some use it to explain away any interpersonal friction and the unwillingness or inability to resolve conflict. Others may spin their split-ups as "creative differences" in order to save face; it sounds better than "drug problems" or "squabbles over money." Legitimate creative disagreement is just one of the countless reasons bands split up.

Fans and pundits alike have often accused John Lennon's widow, Yoko Ono, of causing the breakup of The Beatles. Unfortunately, she is probably just as much a victim of the internal group dynamic as John, Paul, George, or Ringo. She happened to be in the wrong place at the wrong time. It's more likely that the real source of the conflict was the death of long-time manager (and "fifth Beatle") Brian Epstein and the subsequent management of the band's business affairs: at the time the leading candidates included McCartney's father-in-law, Lee Eastman, and Rolling Stones' manager Allen B. Klein. The Beatles' breakup was a rare case in which the four members went on to have successful solo careers, but who knows whether the band would have continued on to even greater artistic and commercial heights had they stayed together? Sadly, we'll never know.

Of course The Beatles' breakup was famously captured, in part, in the film and album *Let It Be* (1970). For better or worse, a number of other films have captured the disintegration of groups over the decades. In *Some Kind of Monster* (2004), the feature-length documentary about the making of Metallica's album, *St. Anger*, tension surfaces between band members for a variety of reasons, including alcoholism, family pressures, and creative direction. Together these issues very nearly split Metallica, although clearly the band survived to play another day. The more recent *Beats, Rhymes & Life: The Travels of A Tribe Called Quest* (2011) depicts the seminal hip-hop collective's split as a result of interpersonal conflict between its members. These are just a few cautionary tales of conflict caught on film.

Although they may attract the lion's share of the media spotlight, pop and rock bands do not have a monopoly on conflict. Jazz great Miles Davis was legendary for his "difficult" temperament and was reported to have a particularly challenging relationship with John Coltrane. When conductor Charles Dutoit left rather suddenly after a quarter century as leader of the world-renowned Montreal Symphony Orchestra, his departure supported the commonly held belief that even the most celebrated and successful orchestras seldom get along well with their conductors. In his memoir, *The Toughest Show on Earth: My Rise and Reign at the Metropolitan Opera*, former Met General Manager Joseph Volpe vividly describes his dismissal of diva soprano Kathleen Battle and offers his rationale for the controversial move.

The good news is that the musical legacies of some contentious partnerships occasionally survive; the bad news is that so many more collaborations never get to reach their full potential.

Groups and duos aren't the only ones to suffer from conflict; solo artists are just as prone, as are the people they work with. Consider the many opportunities for disagreement between a performer and her manager, or between the artist's manager and the record label or publisher. Throw in a producer, studio engineer, A&R representative, orchestra conductor, booking agent, and publicist: the potential for conflict grows proportionately. As long as there are decisions to be made regarding repertoire, recordings, touring, performances, songwriting, marketing, or publishing (to name just a few key areas), there is opportunity for dispute and disagreement. In short, there's plenty of conflict to go around in the music business.

Not surprisingly, it can sometimes get downright litigious: with the advent of peer-to-peer MP3 file sharing, the record labels even began suing their best customers, the fans. Sadder still are those world-renowned artists, ranging from Van Halen to The Doors to Guns N' Roses, who have had their legacies sullied by bitter and long-running legal battles over "selling out" to commercial interests or the use of trademarked band names. Once conflict sets in, it can seem hopelessly irreversible, and undoing the damage caused can be equally daunting. It's particularly tragic when the conflict is allowed to fester until a band member passes away, making reconciliation impossible.

If all of this sounds depressing, take heart: not all conflict is irreversible. There can, in fact, be tremendous value in healthy, *productive* conflict. A good song can be made great by the conscious, effective use of creative tension. For proof, just listen to the collected works of The Beatles, or The Clash, or any one of a thousand other acts whose timeless classics have been the result of collaborative efforts. Critics have written volumes about the contrast between John Lennon's and Paul McCartney's contributions to The Beatles, for example, or the complementary styles of The Clash's Mick Jones and Joe Strummer. Often it's only once a duo or group really engages in substantial (and sometimes heated) debate that all parties can walk away satisfied that the work is truly the best it can be.

Conflict may be necessary to create wholehearted "buy-in," which is more than simple agreement. Without a healthy, productive conflict, commitment to a song, album, or even a band name may be lacking because one or more parties may feel that the ideas haven't been sufficiently road-tested. It's the difference between a half-hearted "Yeah, whatever," and a resounding "Yes!" Even if your creative contributions don't always get chosen, chances are you like to be reassured that they've at least been properly discussed, debated, and maybe improved before being rejected. It's not surprising, however, that few people view conflict as beneficial, because the word is saddled with negative connotations.

The key, as we'll see in this book, is to think about conflict preventively. Most of us only start thinking about conflict once it actually occurs, by which point feelings may be hurt and damage is already done. But it doesn't have to be that way. The challenge is that conflict is pervasive; left unchecked, it inevitably affects your work and influences your behaviour, often in subtle and insidious ways. Any anger or lingering resentment, for example, might leak out unexpectedly and inappropriately.

Think of how you feel when you are internally conflicted; it can make you frustrated, irritable, or unpredictable. Your behaviour can be misunderstood or misinterpreted and perceived by others as annoying or infuriating. Now imagine how you feel with a conflict simmering just below the surface between you and another person with whom you frequently work in close contact: you can begin to appreciate the complex jumble of emotions that can rapidly inflame a situation. The risk of long-term harm to the relationship is real and significant. Looking at the "bigger picture," the real tragedy is that the world may never know just how much great art has been lost forever due to unresolved or unmanaged conflict.

# Who this book is for

We wrote this book for musicians, and other creative, cool people like you. (If you're reading this, you clearly qualify.) Its purpose is to help you and your bandmates—or your significant other, your album cover designer, your manager, your student, etc.—not only *survive* conflict relatively unscathed, but also to *make it work for you* wherever possible. If we can empower you to recognize a conflict for what it is and use tools to manage it consciously, then we will consider it a service to the Muses.

This book is also written for the artist managers, record company executives, music teachers, publishers, and anyone else with whom musicians might come into contact. In fact, as the title says, it's really for any cool people who think creatively and find themselves in conflict with others for any reason at any time.

Realistically, it's not a matter of *if* conflict will happen but *when*. Conflict is inevitable, because even the most wilfully independent creative types can't work in total isolation forever. Whether or not you have the luxury of a solitary creative process, you will eventually need to work with others to market your music and move your career forward. The moment you involve just one more person in any endeavour, there is always risk of conflict. Even if you can agree on most things, the other person(s) will probably have a different

- idea
- perspective
- job or role
- goal or objective
- philosophy or worldview
- belief system
- set of values
- opinion or attitude.

There is so much room for disagreement that the real mystery, as many observers have noted, is not why so many great groups break up, but why more of them don't.

To dismiss conflict as the product of ego is to oversimplify. Egotism is often the stated or implied cause in newspaper or magazine accounts of band breakups, and these generalizations don't help get at the real root causes or find solutions.

A key purpose of this book is to make sure that you can take the necessary steps to minimize the likelihood that a conflict will devolve into a destructive, personal attack, or worse. (Even if the other party doesn't utilize the tools and techniques contained in this book, you can still guide them towards a more satisfactory outcome.) Your work is too valuable—even if the rest of the world doesn't recognize it yet!—to allow it to die as the result of conflict.

Contrary to romantic myth, being miserable does not necessarily make you a better or more prolific songwriter or performer. Misery and depression can instead be one of the many by-products of conflict. Sure, you might think that conflict can provide a little more grist for the artistic mill—temporarily, anyway—but recent research in the field indicates the opposite is true: happiness may instead be the key to enhanced output. So why not lessen your conflict and increase your chance of happiness as well as creativity?

**You may want (or need) to read this book if you are experiencing any or all of the following challenges** (simply replace "band members" with "coworkers," "significant other," or "family members" if you're not a musician yourself):

- trouble communicating effectively with band members
- band members being secretive or withholding information
- frequent groundless arguments and/or displays of insensitivity towards bandmates
- band members taking unreasonably rigid positions in disagreements
- unfair or unwarranted criticism directed at one or more band members

- relations between band members have become noticeably frosty or stiff and formal.

These are symptoms of possible conflict in your group, home, workplace, or indeed virtually any situation involving other people. If conflict is present, this book can help you deal with it more effectively and maintain the relationship while reducing your stress and anxiety levels.

Play on!

# Part I – Some Basic Conflict Theory

By the end of this section, you will be able to

- differentiate between disagreement, conflict, and harassment or bullying
- evaluate the costs of conflict
- recognize four warning signs of conflict: Emotional—Physical—Behavioural—Relational
- determine when it's appropriate to get help managing or resolving a conflict
- assess and evaluate a conflict situation
- distinguish between the types of conflict resolution assistance available
- locate resources for assistance with conflict resolution.

## Conflict: A signal that something needs to change

Conflict is a word we hear a lot—it's in the news practically every day—but don't necessarily think about. What does it really mean? And, more importantly, what does a person mean when they say, "I'm in a conflict with my bassist/vocalist/drummer/etc."? Ironically, there is no single, universal definition of conflict. There are definitions in encyclopaedias, and you can look it up in other books about conflict, but you will soon find that there isn't one common meaning of the term. So, for the purpose of this book and your musical journey, we are going to define conflict as follows: it's simply *a signal that something needs to change*, either between individuals or in a given situation.

By defining it this way, we hope to do two things, the first of which is to take some of the emotional heat out of the term. People fear conflict, often with good reason. But don't let anxiety control you or make you avoid conflict completely; as we'll soon explain, some conflict can actually be good for you! Our second goal is to let you know that there is hope in conflict and that it doesn't necessarily mean the end of your band. On the contrary, it simply lets you know that something needs to be fixed before you can move on.

You know that moment when you are listening to your new composition and it doesn't sound quite right? Those are musical signals telling you that something needs to change in the song, whether it's a chord, a melody line, or a harmony. It's the same idea with conflict: it's a signal telling you that something in a relationship, or in a situation, needs to shift. In other words, the personal or situational harmonics are off. It doesn't mean that the whole song (or your co-writer!) is wrong and that you have to trash the tune or break up the band.

Moreover, the mere fact that there is a conflict doesn't tell the whole story; it's just a symptom of something else. The bigger picture includes *how* you got to this point and what happened that led to the issue. Somewhere along the way, something has gone wrong between you and another person, or with the situation you are in, and now you find yourself in conflict. Something needs to change or the conflict will continue, and maybe worsen.

Imagine meeting four band members in conflict. They are at the point where they might say, "Yeah, it's pretty bad, we're thinking of going our separate ways." Clearly this conflict didn't randomly appear one day in the middle of band practice. Rather than shrug and accept the split as inevitable, you'd probably ask the group, "Where did the conflict come from? What factors led up to it? Surely it wasn't spontaneous."

"Well, of course not," they would probably answer. "We had different ideas about where we should go with our new recording. We tried to work it out at first, but we couldn't, and things just went downhill from there."

The fact that they ended up in a conflict tells you that something went off the rails between them somewhere along the line. The clash of ideas for their new album just means one or more band members found something fundamentally dissatisfying about the band's process, such as:

- how they handle creative differences
- how they make decisions
- how they talk about difficult subjects
- how they collaborate
- how they react to triggers such as ego, control, respect, etc.

In this example you can see that conflict is really just a sign that *how this band has been handling some aspect of its relationship, or how it has been dealing with this situation, needs to change.* After all, if it was a simple disagreement and nothing needed to change then there would be no conflict.

The same is true for you and your band (or the band you manage, the artist[s] on your roster, etc.): conflict is simply a sign that there needs to be a shift in your relationship or in the particular situation. That's all! It's not fatal. The real challenge comes when conflict goes unmanaged and escalates.

Having defined conflict as simply a signal that something needs to change, it's useful to differentiate it from other states that are potentially more damaging.

## The Difference between Disagreement, Conflict, and Bullying/Harassment

There are three terms that people tend to use interchangeably: *disagreement, conflict,* and *harassment* (of which *bullying* is one form). Depending on how riled up you are, you might use any one of these words to describe the current state of affairs. But it's useful to make a distinction, because there is a difference between what these words actually mean and, consequently, a difference in how to deal with each situation most effectively.

To distinguish these terms, let's place disagreement, conflict, and harassment on a continuum of pain or emotional distress. It might look like this:

<----------------------------------------------------->

OK         Disagreement     Conflict     Harassment
(normal)

It's important to note that this continuum is *not* a time line: situations that are OK don't necessarily become disagreements over time, disagreements don't always become conflict, and conflict doesn't always turn into harassment eventually. This can and does happen, but only under certain conditions. Remember, it's a continuum of *emotional discomfort*, which means that a disagreement can be quite uncomfortable, but it doesn't feel anywhere near as upsetting as out-and-out conflict does; and even those very unpleasant feelings don't compare to harassment (or bullying), when people can experience violation or feel fear, extreme powerlessness, and so on.

It's important to know the difference between these states, because if you understand what has to happen in order for a disagreement to become a conflict, and for conflict to become harassment, then you can use that knowledge to prevent things from getting worse. The harsh reality is that if a disagreement is not handled well it *can* escalate into conflict, and a conflict that remains unresolved *has the potential* to turn into a harassment situation. Clearly neither are desirable outcomes, but going down that road is very much within your power to prevent.

On the far left of the continuum, when everything is *OK* between people (a normal, non-conflicted state), there is no problem: conversations carry on as normal and the level of emotional distress is at zero. All is good and everyone's in their happy place. But sometimes issues arise; stuff happens. When problems surface, you usually try to work them out early on in the game. It isn't always easy, but you try. And in the process of trying to work them out, if you find yourselves stuck but still fundamentally getting along, then that's a disagreement. You might differ on something, but *you* are still good—in other words, your relationship is intact. You still like, trust, and respect each other. As the cliché goes, you simply agree to disagree. It's nothing personal.

*Conflict* is different. Conflict means that you are likely in disagreement over a particular issue and, furthermore, something has happened between you and the person with whom you have the disagreement. Depending on how serious that something is, your relationship has probably sustained some damage; things have been said and you are hurting, feeling negatively towards each other. Trust is on shaky ground. Respect is faltering. The situation has become personal. Emotions are running high(er), and phrases commonly heard in situations like this include, "You betrayed me," "You have ruined things," "Obviously you don't care," "You never listen," "You do this all the time," "I don't give a shit anymore," "I'm getting sick of this," "I'm so pissed off/hurt/disappointed/frustrated," etc. Conflict is a very different—and stronger—state than disagreement, so conflict rates higher on the continuum of emotional distress.

*Harassment* (along with *bullying*) is something else altogether. With harassment, there doesn't need to be a pre-existing disagreement, and there may not even have been an initial conflict between the parties. Instead, someone might have exhibited a behaviour that you find offensive—for example, persistent jokes about your playing—and despite asking them several times to stop, they continue. Perhaps someone is using social media to deliberately humiliate you or intentionally sabotage your reputation. Maybe someone has some information on you and is using that power to intimidate you. Or it might be that someone has acted contrary to a law or policy, such as discrimination or sexual harassment.

Regardless of the specifics, harassment can be defined as some sort of violation of a person's human rights. If you are dealing with a situation at the harassment level, then please get help from someone with experience in this area who can give you the advice and support that you need. This person may be a professional of some kind or a wise and trusted friend or colleague—whatever works for you—but do get that help. (We'll discuss when to get help, what kind to get, and where to get it, later in Part I.)

Returning to our continuum of emotional distress, you can see how each one of these states, from *OK* through *harassment*, feels quite different, and each of these terms means something just as distinct.

Now that you know the terminology and the basic differences between these states, you have just increased your awareness of how to prevent things from going south. In a nutshell, if you find yourself in a disagreement with someone, *keep focused on the issue*—that is, the *thing* that needs to be fixed. Don't let it become personal! In other words, avoid shifting the focus from *what* needs to be fixed, to *who* needs to be fixed. Once the parties in a disagreement begin talking about what's wrong with each other, instead of the problem central to the conflict, they have just made things worse and much harder to resolve.

The good news, however, is that subsequent sections of this book will give you many valuable tools you need to productively deal with disagreements when they arise, to keep them from becoming personal, and to prevent disagreements from escalating into conflicts. You will learn basic techniques and skills for resolving many different types of conflict.

# The costs of conflict

One thing is sure: conflict that goes unresolved or is poorly managed can be expensive on many levels. The obvious example of the costs of conflict is war: trillions of dollars are spent funding the military machine, to say nothing of the costs associated with so-called "collateral damage." This includes the loss of lives, shattered individuals, destroyed families, ruined health, devastated communities...the list, unfortunately, is long. That's often the way it is with lesser conflicts, too, like the ones we encounter in our day-to-day lives.

When conflict is not resolved, or at least isn't handled well, there are always costs attached. Although it's hard to find accurate figures (because the costs are largely hidden), conflict is the single most preventable expense in the workplace. In fact, in 2005, Section 207 of the Canadian Public Service Labour Relations Act (PSLRA) made it mandatory for all federal government departments and agencies to have a mechanism in place whereby employees could access alternative dispute resolution (ADR). This was because the costs of harassment and grievance complaints for Canada's single largest employer (i.e., the Public Service) were shown to be greatly reduced when conflict resolution mechanisms were made available. In family life, the damage of conflict extends far beyond the financial, often resulting in broken families with one or both parents stressed out and their children traumatized. Conflict in the arena of politics can result in terrible decisions that adversely affect not only the human population, but the natural world as well.

Conflict in the entertainment industry produces all kinds of unwanted drama, and the more pricey extremes can include contract terminations and the dissolution of creative and business partnerships, to cite just a few examples. When it comes to the music industry, the costs of conflict are enormous—and possibly surprising. A selective list would include:

- *Absences due to stress/health.* Record companies, publishing companies, bands, management companies and agents—to name just a few major categories of those affected—all suffer to varying degrees from the hidden costs associated with conflict. Some cases of absenteeism can be directly attributed to a person's unwillingness or inability to deal with someone else at work, while many others are caused by the manifestation of genuine physical symptoms related to stress, such as headaches, nausea, or other aches and pains. Band members can also suffer from stress and health-related absenteeism. It may be, for example, that the reason one of your band members is chronically late or missing is not due to substance abuse but to the desire to avoid conflict. (Another possibility is that apparent drug or alcohol abuse is actually a symptom of a larger problem and is a coping mechanism to deal with stress and anxiety around conflict.)

- *Related health issues.* The cost of counselling to help overcome the fear and anxiety attached to a particular workplace conflict can be prohibitive, as can the cost of dealing with the physical symptoms of stress and anxiety as outlined above. Visits to the doctor, physiotherapy, medications...it all adds up.

- *Confusion or disruption of band roles.* Some band members might relinquish certain key duties, like booking gigs or renting rehearsal space, if they lead to conflict. Some conflicts might result in band members being stripped of certain voting rights or other privileges.

- *Sabotaged or destroyed work.* In fits of anger, some musicians have been known to erase or alter recordings. In a dispute with their original record company, EMI, British band Dexys Midnight Runners once stole and effectively held hostage the master tapes for its much-anticipated second album. Gigs may need to be cancelled if a band member walks out in the wake of an unresolved or poorly managed conflict.

- *Reduced productivity.* Conflict drains energy and can waste valuable rehearsal or writing time. Not surprisingly, bands find their output diminished when faced with conflict.

- *Loss of skilled band members.* Countless bands have suffered the departure of valued members, often to the lasting detriment of all involved. At the risk of sparking debate over aesthetics and/or commercial success, we suggest that The Velvet Underground lost a vital ingredient to their signature sound when John Cale left; Roxy Music was never quite the same without Brian Eno; and The Clash all but ended shortly after Mick Jones departed. These are just three of countless examples where the loss of a group member resulted in a change of fortune. It could be argued that some lineup changes are beneficial in the long run, but certainly not all. The key question is whether it is a risk you and your group are willing to take.

- *Auditioning and orientation of new band members.* In the business world, it's common knowledge that recruiting, "onboarding," and training new hires is one of the most expensive processes undertaken by human resources practitioners, especially if the new recruits don't survive the probationary period. The same is true with bands; it takes a lot of time, effort, and patience to find and induct a new band member with just the right look, sound, attitude and/or musical pedigree.

- *Loss of creative ideas.* Conflict can drain valuable creative energy or lead to band members withholding ideas and input, especially if they fear conflict arising in the wake of their contributions.

- *Inferior quality decisions.* Decisions that are made in haste just to "get it over with," or made while one or more band members' input is being withheld, are almost always ones that don't last. Equally questionable are decisions made when one faction "gangs up" on another to outvote them. (Later we'll see that conflict, managed productively, can actually be crucial to getting the best quality decisions out of a group.)

- *Unproductive or inefficient brainstorming.* Similarly, the quality of any creative activity—such as coming up with a band name or album title, or jamming away to develop song hooks—suffers as a result of conflict. It's easy to imagine an unhappy player keeping her best ideas to herself "just in case" the band breaks up and those ideas are needed for a solo album or the next band.

- *Damaged relationships at home/in society or community.* A conflict might originate inside the band (or organization), but conflicts have a habit of "leaking out" into other domains of a person's life. We call this the "wallpaper bubble effect," and if you've ever tried to lay wallpaper, you know how it works: suppressing an air bubble in one area under the wallpaper only causes it to pop up elsewhere. A similar thing happens with anger or any other emotion that might be suppressed in a conflict; it's hard to keep it from manifesting in other areas of your life, including your primary/romantic relationship, at home, or in your community.

- *Tarnished reputation.* Bands that are renowned for their infighting don't make good candidates for major record label recording deals. Constant conflict signals that a band is probably difficult to deal with, full stop, and in a buyer's market it's easier to bypass troubled acts in favour of others that have their poop in a group, to coin a phrase. Bands with "revolving door syndrome" due to frequent personnel changes can also find it very difficult to attract or retain new members.

- *Limited (or failed) careers.* Left unmanaged or unresolved, conflict can also spell the end of an entire career: the breakup of Oasis, the Smiths, or The Beatles (among countless others) comes to mind. Even the loss of a single member due to conflict can bring about a permanent change in a group's musical chemistry and, with it, the end of the collective creative DNA that made the band so special.

- *Disappointed fans and clients.* There's only so much that even the most rabid fan will tolerate; eventually they will move on and find another artist to follow, whether or not the band breaks up. If the creative output suffers as a result of conflict, that's another reason fans might abandon their favourite artists. The same is true for organizations: customers and clients will find another firm to do business with if the conflict affects the quality of their product or service.

- *Threats to safety.* If things get bad enough and all civility breaks down, personal safety and security can be a casualty of conflict. Violence is not unknown in the music industry and, as outlined previously in the Brief History of Conflict section, it can happen onstage as well as off.

Clearly, unresolved or poorly managed conflict will cost you money, time, relationships, and, perhaps worst of all for everyone, great music. Remember, it doesn't have to be this way. If you deal with conflict as soon as you notice there is a problem, your chances are better than average that matters will be resolved successfully. This means that the situation won't get worse, you will save yourself lots of stress and anxiety, and the music will continue.

Another very important thing will happen when conflict is dealt with early on: your fellow musicians (and other cool, like-minded people) will learn from the experience and grow. Best of all, on a personal level, you will get better at preventing conflict and at handling it positively and productively when it does occur. Like any other skill—including writing or playing music—conflict resolution gets better with practice. Eventually you will begin to be known for your leadership skills in this area, and you will develop a reputation in the industry as someone who is pleasant to work with. Given the choice between a musician with excellent chops but no people skills and a musician with less than perfect musicianship but lots of leadership skills, most people would prefer to work with the latter. And what musician doesn't want more opportunities?

Now you know why you will want to address conflict as soon as you realize something is amiss: the costs of not doing so are obvious, and far too high.

Next, we'll take a look at some of the signs that will tell you it is time to act.

## The Four Warning Signs: Emotional, Physical, Behavioural, Relational

The first step in resolving, or at least managing, conflict is simply to recognize when conflict may be occurring. This sounds like an obvious statement, but when you really think about it, it's usually far easier to become engulfed in a conflict than it is to be aware it's happening.

The earlier you can detect the signs of an emerging conflict, the sooner you can take steps to resolve or manage it effectively and prevent further harm. Recognizing these signs provides insight into what's happening with you personally. You can also use them to observe what's happening with others (like your fellow band members) and take appropriate action.

Conflict starts somewhere; it doesn't just arrive, spontaneously and fully formed, out of the clear blue sky. The first warning signs that something's wrong come from within; they're **emotional** signs. If they go unrecognized or ignored they will eventually spiral outward and manifest externally as **physical** warning signs. If the outward signs are overlooked they will transform into **behavioural** signs and, if they too are left unchecked, will eventually result in **relational** signs. It's as if something (or someone) is trying to tell you something, and goes to increasing lengths to get your attention.

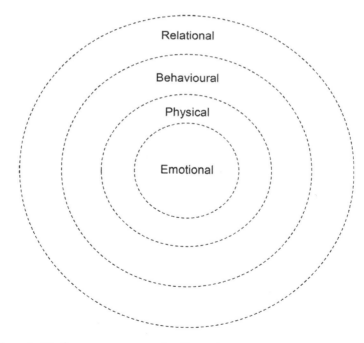

*Figure 1: The four warning signs of conflict radiate outward.*

Let's take a look at what each of these mean and why they happen.

## Emotional signs

The first signs that something is going awry for a person—or perhaps a group of people—are internal: *emotions*. Feelings are a reliable barometer, letting you know when things aren't OK. If the baseline, or normal, is a state of comfort, happiness, relaxation, engagement, calm, and/or contentment, then you can usually soon tell when you move away from that baseline. You can readily identify or describe any *un*happy feelings you're having. When trouble is brewing between you and another person, these unhappy feelings are going to be the first indications that all is not quite right. Pay attention to them.

These feelings will, of course, vary according to each individual involved and each situation. One person might find a particular situation humorous or sad while another might react with anger. The same person might even experience different feelings in a similar situation if some of the specifics change (for example, a situation that might seem humorous when it happens to someone else is usually not so funny when it happens to you!). The intensity of the feeling might also vary from one instance to the next. You might feel confused if you have multiple feelings simultaneously. The list of possible emotional reactions is long. There is no "right" or "wrong" feeling or combination of feelings; what's most important to remember is that *any feeling at all that is outside the normal comfort range is a warning.*

Whatever they may be, these feelings should not be ignored or repressed. Some find it easy to overlook them because society tends to avoid expressing unpleasant feelings or at least disregard what's going on inside when we experience them. Whether or not you choose to divulge them, it's important to recognize that these feelings are a kind of gauge indicating to you whether or not the person you are dealing with, or the situation you are in, is psychologically healthy and safe. They're like the VU (volume unit) meters on a mixing board: when they're pushing into the red zone, you know the signal is "clipping" and you need to do something or there will be unwanted noise and distortion introduced into the signal. If your emotional VU meter is tipping into the red when you are with a particular person or in a specific situation, pay attention, because that's your psyche trying to take care of you. It's sending a red alert, telling you something is off and you need to take care of yourself.

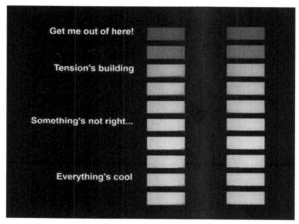

*Figure 2: The emotional VU meter.*

Sometimes taking care of yourself simply means stepping away from the person or situation causing the discomfort, taking a time-out, and putting some distance between the two of you. That may be all you need for your emotional barometer to return to its baseline and for you to once again feel calm, relaxed, engaged, happy, or whatever your normal state happens to be. If that's genuinely the case—you have a good night's sleep, the feelings are gone the next morning, and you haven't simply repressed them or avoided expressing them—then it probably means you don't actually have conflict.

If the feelings persist, however, it could mean there is a problem between you and that other person. Again, we have a tendency to want to sweep unhappy feelings under the proverbial rug, to mask them and avoid dealing with them openly. But they frequently signal the beginnings of conflict, and at this point the onus is on you to deal with the situation and not simply ignore the emotional signs, hoping they'll go away. Trying to "rise above" or "be professional" about the uncomfortable situation are two of the many ways we cope with unpleasant feelings. But when there is a genuine conflict between two or more people—one in which the relationship is being challenged (if not damaged) in some way—then the feelings are not going to go away on their own. Remember, emotions serve as defence mechanisms to let you know when the person or situation may not be psychologically healthy and safe for you, and it would be dangerous to ignore or downplay them.

## Physical signs

If the emotional warning signs (feelings) are ignored, another natural protective mechanism kicks in. The manifestation of *physical* warning signs is your psyche saying to you, in effect, "I tried to warn you! You didn't pay attention, and since my job is to make sure you're going to be okay, I'm going to send you a second set of signals that are more difficult to ignore."

Again, since everyone is different, people will experience physical warning signs of conflict differently, but some symptoms are quite common. Some may be as simple and seemingly innocuous as nervousness or sweaty palms. Other symptoms are more noticeable and worrisome. For example, you may find that you have trouble sleeping. The tossing and turning, the waking up at two a.m. and not being able to fall back sleep again, are common signs. The opposite may also be true: you may find that you begin to sleep more than usual as a way of escaping from the conflict or to help recover from the stress and anxiety it brings. These are two opposite but equally valid physical signs that can be harder to ignore than emotions, precisely because they affect not only your mind but your body.

Another early warning sign of conflict is what we are going to call physical depression, as distinct from emotional or chemical depression. This means you typically find yourself with low energy, dragging your feet throughout the day after hauling yourself out of bed, and this pattern repeats no matter how much quality sleep you get. This is because it takes a lot of physical as well as emotional energy to cope with the demands of conflict on your body. You might also find that you experience an increase in headaches that are often brought on by prolonged stress and anxiety. Other physical warning signs of conflict may be things that you are doing physically, like smoking, eating, or drinking more than usual. Subconscious strategies like these allow us to have physical sensations that mask the other unhappy feelings we may be experiencing, however temporarily.

Unfortunately, the physical warning signs have their own knock-on effects, especially when piled on top of the emotional stuff. Consider the consequences of eating, drinking, or smoking to excess, for example. The short-term results may be stomach aches, hangovers, or smoker's cough, and the longer-term consequences can be far more severe, even deadly. Remember, if you have been experiencing any of these physical symptoms, it probably means the original problem hasn't gone away of its own accord, and the purpose of the physical signs is to make the warning harder to ignore so that you'll finally be moved to do something about it and take care of yourself. Ideally the care-taking will occur before even worse things happen.

Even sleeping too little or too much can have consequences extending beyond the physical. In workplace scenarios, the result of unmanaged conflict is typically an increase in chronic lateness or absenteeism. This brings us to the next set of warning signs.

# Behavioural signs

If the physical warning signs of conflict go unheeded long enough—that is, if an individual chooses to carry on, not necessarily wallowing in emotional and/or physical misery but still not dealing with the core issue—then the clever psyche sends another set of signals. Now, however, these *behavioural* signals are so overt, they can be observed by other people. It's as if your subconscious is saying, "I'm going to issue another cry for help, and this time you won't be able to ignore it because it will show up in a way that others will notice." The logic behind this subtle strategy is this: if you can't (or won't) take care of yourself, you will get someone else to do it for you.

How does your subconscious enlist others in your conflict caretaking? Here, too, everyone is different but some of the more common tell-tale behaviours include the following:

- a normally calm and serene person begins acting agitated and on edge

- a typically patient person becomes short-tempered and easily triggered

- an otherwise engaged and outgoing person begins withdrawing

- etc.

More specifically, you might notice, for example, that a band member who usually goes out socially after band practice starts making excuses to go right home, or one who can normally be counted on to participate in band discussions and decision-making stops contributing. They may just shrug and say, "Whatever. I don't care." Conversations likewise become more difficult, more tense, more strained. Text or Facebook messages may take much longer to get answered, if they're answered at all—or perhaps the responses are shorter and more tersely worded than usual. Eye contact with others may be avoided, and so on. You don't need to be an expert at conflict resolution to detect them; even the untrained eye can usually spot subtle behavioural signs.

Of course, these abnormal behaviours could be symptoms of some other issue or problem, but it's a good bet that the thing bothering your bandmate is conflict. You won't know for sure unless you ask. Even then, it's possible that they won't respond (at least not immediately or candidly), but generally when someone starts acting outside the norm in terms of what they say, how they say it, or even how much they say, it's probably some sort of cry for help. A display of unusual behaviour will likely prompt others to ask, "What's going on?" In this sense it's a kind of invitation to help—not a very articulate or direct one, perhaps, but an invitation nonetheless.

Naturally, these uncharacteristic behaviours draw others in and begin to affect other people. As a result, they also affect the relationship between those involved. This brings us to our fourth and final set of conflict warning signs.

# Relational signs

*Relational* warning signs are, quite simply, those that manifest in the way that people relate to each other. Since these four categories of indicators radiate progressively outward, increasing in their visibility to others and in their impact, the relational signs are the most difficult of all to ignore because they're the most public. Like the other three sets of signals, they also tend to make themselves known if the preceding warning signs go unheeded for too long. And, like the other three categories, they may also appear different for everybody, since no two individuals, conflicts, or situations are identical.

Still, there are some common relational warning signs. A person feeling uncomfortable or in conflict may avoid specific people, mostly the person(s) with whom they are in conflict. In an office setting, this might mean he or she takes a different route to the cafeteria or the washroom in order to avoid the hall where the other party's office is located, so they don't accidentally run into the person around whom they feel uncomfortable. They might ask the boss to put them on a different team so as to not have to interact with the other person. There are many variations on this avoidance behaviour that people typically employ when in conflict, but they might be hard to spot precisely because the avoidance keeps them out of sight and out of mind.

Conversely, the relational warning signs can be easier to detect than some avoidance behaviours because they're much more noticeable. For example, in the context of a band meeting, a musician (or manager, tech crew member, etc.) who has been ignoring his own emotional and physical warning signs too long – let's call him Frank – may be deliberately unresponsive towards the person with whom he is having difficulty, who we'll call Tom. The opposite may also be true; instead of the silent treatment, Frank may begin to single Tom out, making rude or snarky comments in response to his opinions and input or belittling Tom's perspectives and contributions. Frank may be quick to shoot down Tom's ideas. He will openly disagree, challenge, or argue with Tom. When Tom speaks, Frank may roll his eyes, cross his arms defensively, or deliberately begin shuffling pieces of paper or tuning his instrument. Frank may engage in distractions to demonstrate disrespect or otherwise show that he isn't listening or taking Tom seriously. Or Frank may start engaging in rumour-mongering, trading idle gossip about Tom behind his back. Another common strategy is to complain to others in an effort to win sympathy and support.

Through your own prior experience, you may already be familiar with the wide range of actions that signal danger in a relationship. It's important to note that by this point, the behaviours impact not only the person who has been ignoring his or her own internal/emotional warning signs, but clearly *they also start to impact the others in the group, team, or company*. More people are forced to get involved when the behaviour starts affecting them, too. Soon the bystanders will be thinking, "Hey, wait a second, this is becoming a problem for me, too. This is not okay, and I don't want to work in a toxic environment." The stakes are higher now, and if things don't get resolved, soon the whole workplace gets involved one way or another.

## What do the four warning signs mean?

These, in a nutshell, are the four levels of warning signs that conflict is taking place: emotional, physical, behavioural, and relational. In conflict, people seldom stop to take stock of a situation or retrace their steps to figure out how they got to the point where they're no longer willing to talk to each other. But as long as you're aware of these early warning signs, you can remain alert to the fact that something is happening *right now* that's worth paying attention to; something's wrong, and your mind and body are asking you to do something about it. The warning signs tell you it's time to take care of yourself in some way, and the longer you put off taking action, the more intense the signals will become. Invariably they will become more open and obvious, too.

Of course people are often uncomfortable talking openly about their feelings; some families and even cultures are so ill at ease about feelings, they seldom, if ever, discuss them. Some are only comfortable talking about their feelings with therapists or other professionals, because they feel particularly vulnerable. But feelings should be acknowledged and honoured because they have a specific role: to allow you to take care of yourself. Respect your feelings and their noble purpose. Negative feelings are just a sign that something needs to be fixed. Like any bodily sensations, if you ignore your feelings, hoping they'll go away, the symptoms may only get worse over time. If you don't deal with the conflict warning signs promptly, you may eventually find yourself using another, uglier "F-word" in your conversations.

## When Should I Get Help?

Conflict is never fun or easy, and often the first instinct is to seek help. Sometimes help is recommended, but it's not always necessary if you have the core skills. This book is meant to equip you with the fundamental knowledge and tools to prevent most disagreements from escalating and to navigate your way through any existing conflicts. Part of dealing with conflict successfully, though, is having the ability to discern when it is appropriate for you to try resolving a conflict on your own and when you should get assistance. To do this, we need to dispel a couple of widely held myths, more specifically, some misperceptions about getting help with conflict resolution.

# Four myths of conflict

There are four main ideas that commonly inhibit people from seeking help with conflict:

**Myth #1: If I can't deal with this conflict on my own, that must mean there's something wrong with me.** The reason this is entirely untrue is because conflict prevention and resolution skills are exactly that—skills. All proficiencies, just like playing an instrument, sight-reading music, or using a digital audio workstation, are learned and mastered over time. If you didn't succeed at resolving conflict the first time (or few times) you tried, congratulations! You're normal. There is nothing wrong with you.

Unfortunately, people are not born with conflict resolution skills; they have to acquire them. Sure, some seem to have an innate ability to grasp these skills more readily than others, just like some people appear to be born with perfect pitch—but they are still specific skills that require effort to discover, learn, practice, and improve. So, if you don't think you are good at resolving conflict, it's not because Myth #1 is true; it is simply because most of us never acquire and develop these competencies.

Think about it: when you were a child growing up, what kind of conflict resolution skills did you learn in your family environment? How was conflict handled at home? The vast majority of us would probably say that sibling or parental conflict was met with denial, punishment, authoritarian rules, yelling and fighting, and so on. What about at school—were conflict resolution skills part of the curriculum? How about as a teenager—did anything change to provide you with conflict resolution skills moving forward through life?

The sad truth is that only a tiny minority of adults took the time and effort to make sure children knew how to successfully work through conflict by the time they left home. (Don't blame them; that's probably how they were raised, too.) It's more than likely you were taught instead to defend yourself, to stand up to others. For most people, school experience with conflict can be summed up in a few words: Detentions. Suspensions. Bullying. Peer pressure.

Have you ever heard of a high school dialogue club? Probably not, but most of us have encountered a high school debating club. That's because as a society, we value debating—which is essentially the skill of *winning arguments*. Dialogue, on the other hand, is essentially the skill of *arriving at mutual understanding*, which is a very different thing. Winning arguments may be useful in the short term, but genuine mutual understanding is a far more desirable and helpful long-term solution.

By the time you reach adulthood, you have had very little (if any) education or experience in preventing or resolving conflict. No wonder it's hard! Sending people out into the world without any training in conflict prevention or resolution and then expecting them to play nice with others is a bit like giving a bassoon to a kid who has never touched an instrument and expecting him to join the symphony.

Myth Number 1, therefore, simply isn't true. If you can't deal with this conflict on your own because you don't have the skills to do so, you aren't bad or wrong, and you don't need to be fixed, because you aren't broken. On the contrary, it means you are perfectly normal.

**Myth #2: If I need to get help with this conflict, that means I am weak.** Again, this is untrue. If you need to get help with a conflict, then it simply means you have realistically assessed the situation and determined that it would be a bad idea to tackle it alone. If your intuition and your intellect are telling you that you won't be able to successfully work through this conflict without getting some kind of support or assistance, then you have made a good judgment call. You are not weak—quite the opposite, you are rational, discerning, and strong enough to admit anxiety around the conflict. The key is to follow up and actively seek help. (We'll look at where to go for help in Part III.)

**Myth #3: If I need to get help with this conflict, then I'll be perceived as weak by the other person(s).** Wrong again! Reaching out for support in any difficult situation is an intelligent and self-loving thing to do. If someone is suggesting or telling you that you are a weakling for having to get help in dealing with a conflict, try to have compassion for that person. If human behaviour is the outward reflection of what's inside of a person, it stands to reason that the individual who puts down another for getting help is probably experiencing some internal distress. What he's actually doing is making a judgment about himself, i.e., "I would think *I* must be a weakling if *I* needed outside help" (see Myth #2!). Exercise compassion, do what you need to do to get the conflict resolved, and leave the name-callers to their unhappy fate.

It's also possible that no one is actually thinking or saying that you are weak for having to get help in dealing with a conflict. Perhaps it is only your fear that this will be their judgment. Be open to the possibility that they will be thinking something else, including the idea that your mature handling of the situation is quite admirable (even if they might be unwilling admit it at the time).

Let's say you are a cellist in a twenty-piece orchestra. It has become quite obvious that you and Cellist Number 2 have a personality clash. You don't get along, and everyone else in the orchestra knows it. This is starting to cause disharmony (figuratively speaking) with the rest of the members—they don't appreciate being exposed to the thinly veiled comments between the two of you, and everyone is uneasily waiting for a big blowout to occur. Let's also assume you have realized that the continuation of this conflict is too stressful for all concerned, so you try to have a chat with Cellist Number 2, but, despite your best intentions, it doesn't go well. It seems you irritate her as much as she irritates you. Her parting comment is, "Well, you're the one who's wound up tighter than a piano string, so let me know when you're back on your meds and then we can talk." You find yourself triggered; it gets you so mad you just about put your foot through her cello. You have assessed the situation and concluded that handling it on your own will probably not work.

So, your next step is to approach Cellist Number 2 with a proposal: "How about if we go to our Community ADR (Alternative Dispute

Resolution) Centre and sit down with a volunteer mediator to try and work things out? What have we got to lose? It's free." Now imagine that Cellist Number 2 agrees, and the two of you attend mediation and end up resolving your conflict. As part of the agreement that the two of you negotiated, you let your fellow orchestra members know that you went to mediation, patched things up, and will no longer be inflicting your conflict on the rest of the group.

Far from seeing it as a sign of weakness, it's far more likely that they will deeply appreciate your actions, and you will be considered responsible, mature, and professional. You tackled a situation that most people hate dealing with (i.e., conflict) and for which most have no real training. By getting help to resolve the conflict, you ensured a successful outcome. That's a sign of courage, not weakness! Everyone can breathe a huge sigh of relief and get on with the business of making great music.

**Myth #4: We don't need to make such a big deal out of this— we can just talk and work things out.** This may actually be true; as long as the matter is truly not a major, recurring issue, you probably will be able to just talk and work it out. The key here is not to be too quick to dismiss it as "no big deal." Disputes that haven't already spiralled out of control can be handled well on your own if you remember to keep focused on the issue so that the disagreement doesn't escalate into a conflict. These skills are addressed in Part III. But how do you know whether or not it really is a big deal for yourself or the other person? And what if it *is* a big deal—are being "chill" and having good intentions enough to get you through? Worse still, what if you are just saying things aren't a big deal in order to cover up your very real concerns about the situation and to mask your fear of not knowing what to do about it?

If it really isn't such a big deal (we'll show you how to assess and evaluate conflict shortly), go ahead and grab a beer or a coffee and work it out. Use the skills outlined in this book, and you'll resolve it successfully. Have confidence, and remember that conflict prevention and resolution are skills that require practice. On the other hand, if the matter is truly serious or important in any way, don't think that escaping to the mythological land of Chillax will magically alter reality. And if you're not confident about being able to manage it on your own, plenty of assistance is readily available.

# What Kind of Help Should I Get? Conflict resolution processes

The good news is that there are many helpful processes, models, and approaches in the world of conflict resolution. The bad news is that knowing where to start can be overwhelming. To keep it simple, we've distilled it down to what you really need to know in terms of your options, what they are called, and how they work.

- **Problem solving, aka negotiation.** With this process, which is essentially a decision-making exercise, you and the person with whom you are having the issue sit down together and work things out on your own. There is no third party involvement. You use your skills to understand each other's perspectives and figure out what is not working between you and how to resolve it. You can use everything in this book to help you resolve this conflict on your own through negotiation. Review the skills and the basic conflict resolution process presented in Part III, and go for it!

- **Conflict management coaching:** Let's say your assessment of the conflict indicates that you can probably resolve the issue on your own, but you think you might need to sharpen some of your dialogue and negotiation skills or prepare for unexpected turns or worst-case scenarios. Perhaps you just want to get advice about the conflict from someone before you try resolving it without a third party present. In these cases, conflict coaching is an excellent option. With conflict coaching, a conflict resolution practitioner works with you behind the scenes, mentoring you in any of the particular skill areas required, to better prepare you to approach the other person in an attempt to work through your issues together in a productive and positive manner. All parties in a conflict are welcome to use their own conflict coach(es). You may want to try conflict coaching if you're afraid of letting your emotions get the better of you and saying something to the other person that might offend him or otherwise set him off. Maybe a band mate has been late to band practice several times, and previous attempts at changing the behaviour have been unsuccessful, possibly because they haven't been handled elegantly. A conflict coach might also remind you of the steps to resolving a negotiation fairly; practice brainstorming without judgment; work with you to develop multiple options for a win-win outcome; or guide you in other ways to keep the negotiation friendly, mutually supportive, and low on the emotional VU meter.

- **Facilitation:** With facilitation, a neutral third party is directly involved in the negotiation. This is unlike conflict coaching, where the third party is only indirectly involved and works closely with one party, so is therefore somewhat aligned. The facilitation option is particularly helpful when your assessment of the conflict indicates that there is a trouble spot(s) around one or more of the levels of emotion, trust, history or power—enough so that you anticipate it will be difficult to get through a conversation and resolve the issue without the aid of an outside party. A facilitator is impartial and non-biased, and will assist the two of you in staying on track and in keeping the conversation focused, meaningful, and productive. In other words, a facilitator helps both parties equally with their communication, so that you can get more directly to what needs to be fixed, and fix it. One appropriate use of facilitation might be a negotiation over songwriting credits. This is one area, in our experience, where groups or songwriting partners commonly disagree; it's also where the level of emotion is ramped up a notch or two due to creative pride and, of course, the income potential at stake. (Money is one area where people can get very emotional indeed.) In such cases, the history of conflict may be virtually nonexistent, and the power dynamic may be perfectly equal between, say, two songwriting partners, but tension still surfaces. The facilitator's role here may be to help the parties agree on what constitutes a fair split of credit or royalties on a song—because what might seem fair to one partner may not seem fair to another. One could argue that the main melody constitutes the most important part of a song, while the other might argue that the time it took to write the lyrics and work out chord patterns outweighs the effort required to come up with the melody. In this situation, the facilitator might work with both parties to find some mutually agreed upon standard of fairness, or implement a way to assess and evaluate proportionately the work involved. Note that the facilitator is exclusively interested in the *process* of the negotiation and has no attachment to the *content* or outcome of the negotiation. The facilitator is not aligned with either party. The songwriting partners are still doing the "heavy lifting" in terms of the actual negotiation work and decision-making, and the facilitator is simply there to ensure that the *way* they make decisions is effective. The facilitator might help the partners determine a method for deciding the issues to be discussed, but has no input on the issues themselves.

- **Mediation:** Sometimes your assessment of the conflict will indicate that some or all of the levels of emotions, trust, history, and power are in serious trouble. If that's the case, then you know right away that you need help with more than just communication. You will need a third party to help the two of you navigate through high levels of emotions, help the two of you work to rebuild trust, identify the patterns and dynamics that contributed to the history of this conflict, and tackle any power imbalances that exist between the two of you. Mediation goes way beyond communication issues. In cases like this, a mediator will assist the two of you in dealing with the emotions, trust, history, and power issues. Like a facilitator, a mediator is impartial and unbiased. Once again, the mediator will expect the two of you to do the work to resolve your own conflict, but will take on a more active role in guiding you through a process to help you do that. Because the emotional (and sometimes legal) stakes are always higher when mediation is the appropriate option, most mediations begin and end with some paperwork: a confidentiality agreement typically starts the process, and an agreement on how issues were resolved between the parties ends the process. Mediation is probably approach when there is a disagreement over the use of a legacy act's name, for example. World-renowned artists like Creedence Clearwater Revival and The Doors, to name but two, have had their respective disputes over use of the band name coloured by power imbalances and/or prior history of disagreements. In both cases two or more band members (with concomitant voting power) found themselves in opposition to another band member, and in both cases a lot of potential touring revenue was at stake. Emotions were naturally quite high. The two lawsuits were ultimately settled in court (seldom a happy outcome for anyone, since court cases are typically long, drawn-out and costly), but they might have been more successfully—and more cheaply—resolved through mediation. Subsequent interviews with surviving band members from Creedence and The Doors suggest a great deal of regret over how things were handled, particularly after the death of former bandmates. Bitter legal battles had caused irreparable damage to personal relationships, and as they discovered, patching things up after many years of conflict can be difficult if not impossible.

- **Group intervention:** Sometimes a conflict situation involves more than just interpersonal issues between two or a few people—sometimes it's the whole band, ensemble, orchestra, or even a combination of the musicians and management, administration, etc. In any case, when the whole team is affected, then a group intervention is the appropriate option. A group intervention may or may not include individuals using any of the options described above, but it will certainly address the whole team, whomever that might include. Many chart-topping acts—from Metallica to Bon Jovi, Aerosmith, Audioslave, and R.E.M.—have at various times benefited from some form of group intervention, although not always specifically for conflict resolution. Some groups have worked with psychologists and therapists. A group intervention to address conflict is often a complex process, but for now, here are the basics of what you can expect with a group intervention:

  - The entire team contributes to an assessment of the conflict/current situation.
  - An intervention is designed based on the results and interpretation of this assessment.
  - The success of the intervention is assessed and modified where necessary.
  - A follow-up plan is put into place to ensure that the team remains healthy moving forward.

In summary, problem-solving, conflict coaching, facilitation, mediation, and group intervention are excellent ways to work through conflict and come out of it better than ever. One of the many benefits of these processes is that the responsibility and control of the outcome is always in the hands of the people in conflict. No one tells you what to do, dictates an outcome, or makes decisions for you. You get to figure out what is wrong and fix it! Through these processes people can actually get closer, relationships become stronger, trust is built... and this means that more great music is made.

To figure out whether or not you need to get help in dealing with a particular conflict situation, you will need tools to help you to realistically assess the situation first.

# Assessing a Conflict Situation

To assess any conflict situation as objectively as any subjective person can, there are four key dimensions to consider:

1. Emotions
2. Trust
3. History
4. Power

Let's examine each of these things in turn, beginning with *emotions*. The first thing to asses is your emotional level. Are you still feeling fairly calm about the situation? Mildly annoyed, but not enraged? Disappointed, but not full of anger and blame? If your emotional VU meter (from page 26) is telling you that things are not going well but are not yet off the chart, that's one thing. If your VU is indicating that that you are consistently peaking in the red zone, that's quite another.

What about the *level of trust* between you and the other person? Do you still feel a healthy level of trust in them? Do you have the sense that they still genuinely want the best for you, even if the two of you are in disagreement? Do you believe that they will work for the ultimate good of the band, orchestra, or company? Or are you thinking that they are no longer trustworthy, their own agenda has become their prime concern, and they don't really care how you are doing in the midst of the conflict?

Next, look at the *history* of your conflict. Is this conflict a relatively recent one, in which bad feelings haven't really had the chance to develop? Are other people not yet involved? If they are, have they taken sides? Do you still feel reasonably confident you'll be able to resolve these issues with the right skills and approach? Or, is there a long, ugly history to this conflict, with lots of negativity and resentment built up over time with band members, friends, and others getting fully involved or becoming part of the problem?

Finally, take a look at the *dynamic of power* between you. Do you feel that it is fair and balanced? Does the other person have some sort of power or authority over you in terms of their influence or decision-making ability? (Consider, for example, your role in the group; are you a founding member or a hired session player? Do you write all of the songs, or none? Does one member own or control the rehearsal space, manage the band, and/or or pay the bills? These are just some of the factors that may contribute to power imbalances in a group. If the conflict is with your manager, then he has a legal, fiduciary duty towards you—but may also have a tremendous power advantage.) Do you have any concerns about expressing yourself honestly or fears about asking for what you want? Do you find that you muzzle yourself and avoid speaking up, worried that it will make things worse for you because of the other person's power, role, status, or authority?

The trick when trying to decide whether you will need some help in dealing with this conflict (and what kind) is to figure out where you are with respect to emotions, trust, history, and power. If all of these things are in reasonably good shape, you'll probably respond by either trying to manage it yourselves, or by seeking some conflict management coaching or other unobtrusive assistance.

If one or more of these key dimensions are on sufficiently shaky ground, you'll probably respond differently, by seeking more active, professional help. It is your assessment that will help you determine what kind of help or support you should seek. Table 1 below, the Conflict Assistance Chart, helps you determine what kind of process is most appropriate to your situation. To assess a potential conflict situation effectively, we have prepared a Conflict Assessment Worksheet in the Appendix that you can use to evaluate the emotions, trust, history, and power dynamic at work. (You can download additional copies of these documents for free at the Fifth House Group website, at http://www.fifthhousegroup.com/crfmworksheets.html.)

*Table 1: Conflict Assistance Chart*

| Factor | Coaching | Negotiation | Facilitation | Mediation |
|---|---|---|---|---|
| **Emotions** | Any | Low to Medium | Medium | High |
| **Trust Levels** | Any | Good to Medium | Medium | Low |
| **History** | Any | None or Positive | Some | Some or Negative |
| **Power Imbalance** | Any | None or Some | Some | Yes |

Let's look at some examples of how to assess your conflict situation.

*Scenario #1.* Rob is the bassist in a four-piece rock band. The quartet is still mostly rehearsing in the garage but is starting to book gigs at small local pubs and clubs. Although these early gigs are mainly performing covers of current popular songs, the band ultimately wants to perform its own original material. Rob is the most recent addition to the band's lineup (he's the third bassist in as many months) and as a newcomer thinks that it's really the others' group: the band rehearses in the garage belonging to the guitarist and sibling drummer, and the singer founded the group and created the band's name. On the other hand, Rob has turned out to be a prolific songwriter and has written or co-written the majority of the band's original material since coming on board. The main source of disagreement seems to be the musical direction of the new material; the singer, Steve, prefers a Red Hot Chili Peppers-like sound, whereas Rob has imagined a different vibe. The guitarist and drummer have split allegiances; while they have been friends with Steve for a long time, they also value Rob's contributions and want to keep him in the band, especially after their recent trials. They have no particular leanings musically, as they're both just happy to finally be playing in a band with real potential.

Rob and Steve's disagreement hasn't yet degenerated into personal attacks, but it's increasingly evident in band practice that Rob is getting tired of Steve's frequent exhortations to "Play it like this, not like that." Rob either shrugs and acquiesces to Steve's requests or, on those occasions when he's really adamant about it, sometimes continues to play bass parts in his own way until Steve just stops asking him. Steve, meanwhile, is often heard sighing loudly when he doesn't like Rob's playing style, and he's quick to ask Rob to play the bass in a style more like Flea's.

If Rob were to evaluate the conflict using the worksheet provided, he might score it thus:

| Factor | Coaching | Negotiation | Facilitation | Mediation |
|---|---|---|---|---|
| **Emotions** | Any | **Low to Medium** | Medium | High |
| **Trust Levels** | Any | **Good to Medium** | Medium | Low |
| **History** | Any | None or Positive | **Some** | Some or Negative |
| **Power Imbalance** | Any | **None or Some** | Some | Yes |

In this scenario, Rob could choose to address the conflict himself, through negotiation, without any third-party intervention. This would work well if he prepares himself ahead of time and possibly gets some coaching to make sure he goes in well-supported. Alternatively, he could get some conflict management coaching.

*Scenario #2.* Katrina is a top-tier soprano in the world of opera.

Since arriving in her current home of Gotham for her lead role in a gala production of *Aida*, featuring the city's world-class symphony orchestra, she has been butting heads, figuratively speaking, with the conductor, Richard. Richard is a fairly recent and proud acquisition for the Gotham Orchestra; it made the headlines locally and in the international music press when the Gotham Orchestra's board went to great lengths to buy him out of his previous contract a few months early, specifically to allow him to conduct the ambitious, large-scale interpretation of *Aida*. The show, to take place in an unusual venue (Gotham's football stadium), will be simulcast in high-definition to cinemas in select cities around the world and promises to be a landmark event in both financial and artistic terms.

Katrina, despite her status as a prima diva, hears retirement calling. She is growing tired of touring, and she knows that her vocal cords have only one or two more good years left in them, at best. She wants to go out on a high note, so to speak. The problems began when Katrina failed to show up on time for the very first full-cast rehearsal, due to what she feared might be an oncoming cold. Richard—generally a very amiable person whose no-nonsense rehearsal style is matched by his intolerance of diva-like behaviour—gave her a frosty reception when she finally arrived. True to his working-class, egalitarian upbringing and ideals, he made it plain to the orchestra that not even the star of the show should be above being punctual. From that point forward the two have been scarcely communicating except during rehearsal (very tersely, and often nonverbally), and occasionally through pointed comments in the press.

If Katrina or Richard were to evaluate the conflict using the worksheet provided, they might score it thus:

| Factor | Coaching | Negotiation | Facilitation | Mediation |
|---|---|---|---|---|
| **Emotions** | Any | Low to Medium | Medium | **High** |
| **Trust Levels** | Any | Good to Medium | **Medium** | Low |
| **History** | Any | None or Positive | **Some** | Some or Negative |
| **Power Imbalance** | Any | None or Some | **Some** | Yes |

In this scenario, Katrina or Richard should choose to address the conflict with some third party assistance, likely facilitation. This would work well if they prepared themselves ahead of time with the facilitator, so they both go into the facilitation with the clear goals of listening to understand each other, and communicating in order to resolve the issues before them.

*Scenario #3.* Jeanne is a label manager at a major multinational record company. Her responsibilities include developing national marketing strategies for North American releases by some of the biggest names in music, including one top-grossing touring and recording act managed by Marcus. He's an "old-school" manager who cut his teeth managing arena rock acts back in the 1970s, when outrageous behind-the-scenes antics by musicians—and sometimes their managers—were the rule, not the exception. To Jeanne's eyes, Marcus never really outgrew that phase of his life; he is full of bluster and bile, constantly barking orders at his management team members and anyone else who crosses his path, especially if and when things don't go his way. He is often heard making off-colour remarks. He takes advantage of being overseas in another time zone to call Jeanne in the wee hours of the morning, North America time, to catch her off-guard. When he doesn't like a reply of Jeanne's, he mutters sexist expletives and occasionally threatens to take his acts and leave the label.

Therein lies the essence of Jeanne's problem: Marcus not only manages one of the label's flagship acts, but he also manages a host of other, up-and-coming acts who could mean serious business for the label. Although Jeanne is one of the senior product managers and has risen through the company ranks over many long, loyal years, she is terrified of upsetting Marcus and is equally reticent to ask for help, lest she be seen as not being tough or able to withstand the pressures of a fast-paced, male-dominated industry.

If Jeanne were to evaluate the conflict using the worksheet provided, she might score it thus:

| Factor | Coaching | Negotiation | Facilitation | Mediation |
|---|---|---|---|---|
| **Emotions** | Any | Low to Medium | Medium | **High** |
| **Trust Levels** | Any | Good to Medium | Medium | **Low** |
| **History** | Any | None or Positive | Some | **Some or Negative** |
| **Power Imbalance** | Any | None or Some | Some | **Yes** |

In this scenario, Jeanne would choose to address the conflict with some third-party intervention, likely mediation. Because there are clear personality differences between her and Marcus, a history of conflict, and strong feelings of fear on her part, the issues between them involve more than just communication: there are definite interpersonal and psychological aspects to this conflict.

# Where Can I Get the Help I Need?

One place to go for immediate assistance is our website, www.fifth-housegroup.com, where we have posted numerous articles and other free resources for musicians (and other cool, creative types), including the worksheets used in this book. Another option is simply to search the web, using terms such as "conflict resolution services," "alternative dispute resolution services," "community mediation services," "volunteer mediators [your city here]," etc., and follow those leads. You can search for services in your geographic region specifically, but Google and other search engines such as Bing can also provide geographically relevant sponsored links (advertisements) and regular, non-sponsored results through geolocation.

A third option is to check out your local college or university services—many such institutions now offer courses, certificates, and degrees in the field of conflict resolution, and some also offer free or low-cost conflict resolution services in addition to their academic programs. One thing is certain: if you really want to resolve this conflict, you will find resources out there to support you. If you can pay full fare, you will never have a problem finding a professional conflict resolution practitioner. If you don't have that kind of money, with just a bit of effort, you will be able to find free, low-cost or geared-to-income assistance through the many community-based mediation programs that exist in many parts of the world. Where there's a will, there is a way!

## Summary

Wherever there are two or more people working together, there is room for conflict, even in music, where the notion of harmony underpins every collaboration. Conflict has affected some of the most successful duos, pop groups, and symphony orchestras and has split many promising, young, up-and-coming acts, effectively ending their careers prematurely. The costs of conflict can be enormous, extending beyond the musicians themselves out to the fans and the broader community, and the effects long-lasting.

Conflict isn't mere disagreement. In fact, the right amount of *productive conflict* may be essential to successful musical partnerships. Consider the differences between John Lennon & Paul McCartney's contributions to The Beatles' songs, for instance; without these contrasting ideas, *Sgt. Pepper's Lonely Hearts Club Band* might never have been. But in order to ensure things remain healthy and not destructive, we need to differentiate between disagreement, conflict, and harassment or bullying. We also need to understand how conflicts can escalate—often unintentionally—to prevent them from doing so.

To be effective at conflict resolution, we also need to recognize the four types of warning signs of conflict, which begin with our own inner emotional state and radiate progressively outward to become physical manifestations, inform our behavioural responses, and ultimately affect our relationships. At each level there are signals that alert us to the fact that something is wrong, and the sooner we can recognize them, the quicker and easier we can manage and resolve the conflict.

You can attempt to resolve the situation on your own through negotiation, or if you don't feel confident in your conflict resolution skills or your ability to manage the conflict on our own, you can get help. There are many sources of support available to you, ranging from free or inexpensive resources like books and websites (including the Fifth House Group website), to paid professional assistance from conflict resolution practitioners in your local area.

In such cases it helps to be able to determine when it's appropriate to get help managing or resolving a conflict, and the best approach for your particular situation. You can easily assess and evaluate a conflict situation using four key criteria: the level of emotional intensity in the conflict, the levels of trust and the power dynamic between the parties involved, and the history of the conflict. This information can also help you determine which of several modes of conflict resolution assistance may be most appropriate to you, including (but not limited to) negotiation, conflict coaching, mediation, facilitation, and alternative dispute resolution (ADR) mechanisms.

# Part II - The Inner Mechanics of Conflict

By the end of this section, you will be able to

- analyze the role of feelings in conflict situations and interpret a range of feelings relating to conflict.
- explain the role of needs in conflict and discover the needs of parties to a conflict.
- define and interpret strategies used in conflict situations.
- distinguish authentic feelings from blaming feelings.

## Decoding Conflict: Feelings, Needs and Strategies

What's going on inside of you and me when we are in conflict? This may seem like an odd question, but it's an important one. When we're in conflict, it's hard to keep track of what is happening inside ourselves; it seems like thoughts, feelings, and speech happen so quickly, we get triggered all over the place, and we end up not talking about what we really need to talk about. We might suddenly feel provoked or attacked and feel an urge to fight back. We might not even know what it is that we really need to talk about, only that something is wrong and we feel vaguely uncomfortable. In conflict, all kinds of feelings can overwhelm us, leading us to say things that we might bitterly regret later and do things that, in retrospect, definitely don't help. This section is about understanding what is actually taking place on a personal—perhaps even intimate—level when we are in conflict.

There are three essential components involved in any conflict: feelings, needs, and strategies. *Feelings*, as discussed earlier, are there to indicate that something is not quite right with a given situation. What they're really telling us is that there are *needs* that are going unmet or are being threatened. And when we encounter unmet needs, we apply *strategies* in an attempt to meet or restore those needs. It sounds pretty straightforward; it's simple because all conflict really does boil down to these three basic components. On the other hand, it's complex because most of us aren't aware of what these three things are, what they signify, or how they work.

As with conflict resolution skills in general, most of us have gone through life without ever learning about the true nature of feelings, never mind needs and strategies. So it's not surprising that we end up obeying them reflexively, reacting impulsively instead of pausing to decode them and using their hidden meanings to our benefit. But if we are able to pause long enough to recognize the signals and interpret the feelings, needs, and strategies, then we can access a vast amount of valuable information about ourselves and the other people in our lives. A brief analysis will demonstrate how it all works.

## The Role of Feelings

What are feelings, anyway? Like conflict itself, feelings don't just randomly appear. We may not always appreciate or fully understand them, but they have causes. And as quick as we are sometimes to dismiss feelings, they've actually been critical to the development and survival of human beings as a species. Feelings are an ancient, ingenious, and virtually fail-safe mechanism designed to protect you. They have a very specific function: they exist to keep you in a constant state of vigilance as to whether or not the person(s) you are with, or the situation you are in, is good for you. Fear, for example, is one such powerful device. Fear tells you to back away from a wild animal or avoid excessive heights, keeping you safe from both potential dangers.

Put another way, your feelings tell you at any given point in time whether or not your needs are being met (we'll talk more about those needs shortly). *Fear lets you know that your need for safety and security is somehow being threatened.* To invoke our earlier analogy, your feelings are the VU meter that indicates how you are doing with regard to a person(s) or situation. As long as your feelings are in the green zone, your needs are probably being met; when the meter peaks into the red zone, your needs are in danger.

Let's do a quick experiment: take a moment to think about someone, or a situation, that feels good for you. What kinds of feelings do you have when you are with this person(s) or in this situation? Use the word cloud below to see if any of the words resonate with you with regard to the person/situation you currently have in mind:

*Figure 3: Positive feelings*

Adapted from Center for Nonviolent Communication, Website: www.cnvc.org
Email: cnvc@cnvc.org, Phone: +1.505.244.4041

If you identified any or all of these feelings with the person or the situation you thought about for this exercise, then your feelings are telling you that the person(s) or situation is probably healthy for you. The result of an interaction would be generally positive, and there is little or no threat of physical or psychological/emotional harm. *It means that most of your needs are being met.*

Let's change the experiment: now think about a person(s) or situation about which you have very different feelings—the negative kind. See if any words from the following list are applicable:

*Figure 4: Negative feelings*

Adapted from Center for Nonviolent Communication, Website: www.cnvc.org
Email: cnvc@cnvc.org, Phone: +1.505.244.4041

If you are having these sorts of feelings, especially if you are having them continuously or chronically, then that person(s) or situation probably isn't good for you. The feelings you are experiencing are meant to keep you safe from physical or psychological (emotional) harm. *They mean that one or more need(s) is/are not being met.*

When you think about the spectrum of feelings that humans experience in terms of an early warning system, you can see how important it is for giving us some very accurate and useful information. The feelings alone are a reliable indicator, but when you also consider the *intensity* of the feelings, the safety/security information received is that much more clear and powerful. Just like a person would be foolish to ignore a rapidly dropping gas gauge or fast-rising engine thermometer in a car, this information should be taken seriously if we are at all interested in taking good care of ourselves and each other.

Once again (for the analog fans this time), think of your feelings like a VU meter:

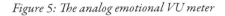

*Figure 5: The analog emotional VU meter*

As feelings gain in discomfort and intensity level, watch out!

## The Role of Needs

We have seen how our feelings act as a warning system to let us know whether the person(s) we are with, or the situation we are in, is generally good or bad for us. But what does "good for us" mean, more specifically? What does it really mean when we decide that "it's good for me to be around so and so," or, "it's a good situation for me to be in"?

On closer analysis, what these expressions fundamentally mean is that in this moment *our needs are being met.*

This begs the question: what type of needs are being met? And what are "needs," anyway? To answer the last question first, needs are *states of being that are essential for (psychological) health, safety, and well-being.*

Before going any further, it's important to make a distinction between *needs* and *wants*, as these terms are sometimes used interchangeably. Remember, a need is essential for psychological health: if that need isn't met, you will experience genuine emotional pain, or in extremely unhealthy situations you might even feel physically uncomfortable. A want is more like a desire—it would be great to have, and sometimes it even seems crucial—but you could, if you had to, live without it. As we shall see later, "wants" are really code for "strategies," but we'll get to that in due course.

In the meantime, know that needs are "non-negotiables" for human beings. Like air, food, water, or shelter, if you take them away, we suffer. Deprived of these, our health and well-being are at risk. But our complex human needs can extend beyond those basic bodily requirements and into more abstract territory. Consider the following list of human feeling-needs:

*Figure 6: Feeling-needs*

Adapted from the Center for Nonviolent Communication. Website: www.cnvc.org
Email: cnvc@cnvc.org, Phone: +1.505-244-4041

If you really think about this list, you can see that these are very real, and they're equally applicable to all of humanity regardless of race, culture, ethnicity, religion, etc. If you're not convinced, imagine yourself stranded on a deserted island. Can you picture what might happen to you psychologically and emotionally if you had to live for a prolonged period of time without any other human contact or connection? Or consider acceptance: if you've ever experienced being ostracized in your life—perhaps you were the new kid who didn't fit in at school, or you were otherwise cast out from the "in" crowd—you know how painful it can be to live without acceptance. Some might argue that you could live forever without appreciation, but, truthfully, if you have ever worked long and hard for something without getting at least a token of recognition for it, then you know how important appreciation really is: without it, you feel emotional pain, and perhaps you suffer. If you've ever been the one to book all the gigs or do most of the heavy lifting at load-ins/load-outs without so much as a thank-you from your bandmates, you know what we mean.

From this perspective, you can see why we call these needs the non-negotiables for human beings. Obviously, everyone has their own set of priorities. Some of these needs will be of less importance to you than others, whereas someone else will prioritize them another way. For one musician, the predominant driving force may be the need to write a great song, while for another the most important consideration may be camaraderie, and for still another the main need is to get recognition.

Fortunately, those of us in the developed nations have most (if not all) of our more basic needs met, so we can afford the relative luxury of spending mental and physical energy seeking to satisfy our higher-order social, personal, and/or self-realization needs. Each of us is unique in our own specific priorities, but we are all alike in that these main categories of needs are equally essential to our personal sense of well-being. Imagine a life where all those base-level needs are not met—what a misery! What would it be like if you had to endure life without ever meeting some or all of the needs associated with Connection in Figure 3?

Now think about the people and situations in your daily life and, more specifically, in your musical career and pursuits. If you think about them from this perspective, you will more than likely recognize that the people and situations that pin your emotional VU meter into the red zone *are those that don't allow your needs to be met.* Here are just a few examples:

- If you feel negatively about a band member showing up late for rehearsals, it may be because you feel your own time isn't valued, since you show up on time and wait around even though you, too, have other things to do and places you could be. You have a need for *respect*, and it isn't being met.

- If you are frustrated over your musical input being disregarded, it may be because you feel you aren't being heard or acknowledged for your contributions. You have a need for *acknowledgement* or *validation* that isn't being met.

- If you are feeling anxious or uncomfortable when group decisions are being made without you (or you're being consistently out-voted), it may be because you feel like you don't belong, or perhaps you feel powerless. Depending on which of these is truer for you, you may have a need to feel *membership* (a sense of belonging) or *agency*—or both!—that isn't being satisfied in these situations.

The key here is to first try to pinpoint exactly what the feeling is, and then identify what is causing it. Yes, the situation or person is somehow contributing to the feeling, but *they're not directly causing it.* The challenge is to remember that no matter how frustrated you might feel, the other person is never the actual problem. If you remember this, you'll help avoid blaming them or being triggered by whatever they might say or do, however inadvertently. (We discuss triggers, and how to avoid them, in Part III.) Instead, the problem is that you have a need that isn't being met. So, what *specifically* is the need that is being threatened, or isn't being satisfied in that situation?

This isn't always an easy question to answer, especially when you're in the midst of a conflict and you are flooded with emotions, thoughts, and judgments. Again, it helps to take a moment to pause and reflect. The more specifically you can identify the feeling, the more accurately you will be able to identify the need—and thus take the necessary steps to get that need met so you no longer have to put up with the negative feelings. But before we get to our discussion of strategies—i.e., how we try to meet our needs—here are a few tips to help identify the underlying need by first identifying the feeling with greater clarity and precision:

**Tip #1: Differentiate between thoughts or judgments and actual feelings.** Often we'll say things like, "I feel like you ignore my ideas." Such statements don't really describe a feeling; ignoring ideas is an *action*, or a behaviour. Therefore that phrase is more of a *judgment* or thought about how the other person is treating you. At worst, the sentence "I feel like you ignore my ideas" can sound like an accusation. **Blaming feelings**, as we like to call them, aren't very helpful, and if they're expressed outwardly they can often worsen the problem by unintentionally escalating the conflict. No one likes to be accused of hurting someone else!

A quick test of whether your feeling is a genuine emotion or an attempt to find fault/lay blame is to note whether you can describe your feeling using only one adjective. If you can complete the phrase, "Right now I feel _____," with a single adjective (e.g., hungry, tired, angry, etc.), then it's probably an **authentic feeling** or emotion. But if you're drawn to complete the phrase with "like," "as if," "you (or he/she/they)," or "that," what's likely to follow is not an authentic feeling. Instead it's likely to be a thought, judgment, or an interpretation of someone else's actions or intentions. Any one of the words below (among others) is probably an indication that what you're expressing is not an actual feeling but is instead a thought or judgment:

*Figure 7: Blaming feelings*

For example, "Right now I feel as if you're ignoring my ideas," or, "I feel like I'm being ignored," "I feel that you're not listening," or any similar variation implies someone else's actions are the problem—in other words, your feelings are somehow their fault.

A more accurate, authentic feeling statement might be, "I feel sad about my ideas not being used," or, "When my ideas aren't used, I feel lonely." Identifying sadness (or anger, loneliness, disappointment, or whatever you're actually feeling) allows others to understand and empathize with what's going on for you internally, and gives you a platform for asking for what you need so that you no longer feel that way.

Having identified sadness or isolation as the real underlying feeling, you're now closer to identifying what you would need in order to no longer feel that way—for example, you might need to be heard, validated, acknowledged, or included as full-fledged member of the band.

**Tip #2: Pay attention to the metaphors and language you and others use.** As tricky as language can be, it can still be useful in pointing to the real underlying feeling. When in the midst of conflict and emotional turmoil, we sometimes resort to metaphors—phrases or idiomatic expressions that serve as replacements or illustrations for something else we may not be able to readily identify in the heat of the moment. So when someone uses a metaphor such as, "I feel like I was left in the lurch," or, "You left me holding the bag," what they're probably trying to tell you is, "I feel lonely," or, "I feel guilty." By decoding the underlying feeling of abandonment or guilt, you've basically recognized the unmet need—the need to feel included as part of the team, or the need to feel vindicated.

**Tip #3: Recognize that frustration is a generic feeling for any need being unmet.** If you can identify a feeling as frustration, then you already know a need isn't being met. The problem is that the feeling of "frustration" could just as easily apply to the need for freedom of artistic expression as to the need for sexual release; so while it's unquestionably a feeling (and not a thought or judgment), it's too a broad term to be very helpful. The trick is to figure out exactly *which* underlying need isn't being met, so you can ask more specifically for what you need. Try, then, to remember what immediately preceded the feeling of frustration, because that will likely point to the underlying need. For example, if a feeling of frustration is immediately preceded by another band member interrupting you, then chances are the real need behind your feeling of frustration is *the need to be heard uninterrupted* (and/or to be respected, validated, etc.).

**Tip #4: Recognize that anger is a secondary emotion.** By this we mean anger is usually preceded by another, primary feeling, which again is the source of the real underlying unmet need. For example, if someone leaps out at you from around the corner of a dark alley and shouts, "Boo!" your first instinctive reaction is usually fear—but it quickly turns to anger, as soon as you realize your life isn't actually in danger. Your next instinct, instead of running away, might be to beat the other person up. (This is a holdover from the primitive safety mechanism all animals have that leads them to either freeze, flee, faint, or fight when confronted by a natural enemy.) The anger is what lasts and what we remember most vividly, so we tend to identify that foremost as the feeling. But you can see how the anger is actually a backup response to one or more of the following primary emotions:

- *surprise* (unmet need: predictability, stability);
- *fear* (unmet need: safety, security);
- *betrayal* (unmet need: belonging, trust);
- etc.

Because anger so universally supersedes and masks other emotions, your initial reaction to the person or situation is a better indicator of the real underlying unmet need.

**Tip #5: Remember that most needs in a conflict boil down to a few common ones.** In a typical conflict situation, if you dig deep enough, you'll discover the underlying needs behind most unpleasant feelings are the needs for belonging and social status, safety or security, respect, acceptance, validation, acknowledgement, recognition, or support. That's not to say that all needs in a conflict can be distilled down to just these few, but they are most common in intra-band conflicts in particular.

To practice identifying the unmet needs in a conflict—whether yours or the other person's—take a look at the table below. Examples are given in the first few rows; in light of what you've just learned about unmet needs, see if you can decode the underlying need for the last few rows:

| If you "feel": | ...then you might need: |
|---|---|
| 1. Stupid | Validation, acknowledgement, recognition |
| 2. Insecure | Security, reassurance, safety, stability |
| 3. Confused | Clarity, decisiveness, calm |
| 4. Ripped off | Fairness, equality, mutuality |
| 5. Helpless | Autonomy, safety, contribution |
| 6. Stabbed in the back | |
| 7. Worthless | |
| 8. In the dark | |
| 9. Left holding the bag | |
| 10. Alone | |

Answers: 6. Feeling: betrayal; Need: security, trust, belonging. 7. Feeling: sadness, disappointment; Need: self-worth, esteem, validation. 8. Feeling: insecurity, confusion, or exclusion; Need: safety/security, clarity, or inclusion, loyalty. 9. Feeling: abandonment, responsibility; Need: togetherness/belonging, support. 10. Feeling: loneliness or abandonment; Need: Togetherness, belonging, inclusion, support.

This table is obviously not meant to be definitive or exhaustive; it is necessarily selective. In more than one case, we deliberately threw you a curve by including some metaphorical language and some thoughts or judgments, just to see if you could discern what the actual underlying feeling(s) and need(s) might be. Note, too, that for each feeling there are a number of possible underlying needs, including ones not listed here. There is seldom (if ever) a single "right" or "wrong" answer; the codes can often be interpreted in multiple ways. If the unmet need is difficult to pinpoint—for either party—then part of your job is to *ask the right questions* to help you discover exactly what need isn't being satisfied.

Questioning is more art than science; it can be a very tricky, advanced skill that is beyond the scope of this book. In the meantime, try the following open-ended approaches to help surface the underlying needs:

- Tell me what your concern is about.
- Help me understand what is important to you about _____.
- Tell me what you were hoping for with regard to _____.

The trick to understanding each other (and staying out of conflict) is to *address the needs that each person is trying to meet*. It's important to understand your own underlying needs, as much as the needs of the other person(s). If you know what you are working with in terms of addressing needs, it becomes much easier to talk together and build solutions that genuinely meet your own needs without threatening or negating the other person's.

If the other party has no idea what the unmet needs are (either their own or yours), it makes sense that they won't be able to satisfy them. They're not mind-readers, but in the midst of the emotional storm, that's easy to forget. We often resort to our own frequently inelegant, awkward, or just plain backhanded strategies for meeting our own needs. The problem is that these poorly executed strategies tend to result in further bad feelings. For example, if one band member is complaining about something, it may simply be that they only want to be heard; but if another band member keeps chiming in with solutions to the problem being complained about, it may only increase the frustration by the complainer. Why? *Because s/he simply wants to be heard*, and not necessarily fixed. (We analyze strategies in more depth in the next section.)

One amazing thing about needs is that human beings are seldom in conflict over them. Needs are always compatible. Look at the list of needs on page 66 again. Can you find two needs that are irreconcilable? In other words, is trust fundamentally incompatible with or opposed to safety? Or warmth vs. beauty, joy vs. discovery, compassion vs. belonging? If you think about these pairs of needs, you can see why it's possible for two or more parties in conflict to each have their needs met without necessarily denying the other(s). They may exist simultaneously, for example, if he needs recognition while she needs respect. They may exist in parallel, as when both parties need the same thing (e.g., validation or belonging). At various times you may find yourself with the very same unmet need as someone else at the very same time. (A common issue in arguments is that neither side feels heard or acknowledged by the other!) The needs may even complement each other (for example, one needs to be heard, while another needs a democratic decision-making process), but they're rarely opposed. For better or worse, we all share these needs.

It's important to stress that the needs themselves are never really in conflict. And clever, creative folks like you can always find ways to satisfy the needs of the parties to a conflict. The trouble really arises between people when their *strategies for meeting those needs* are incompatible. Let's examine those strategies in more depth now, and see why some of them work well while others go awry.

## The Role of Strategies

You now know about feelings and needs, along with their special functions in conflict situations, from a conflict resolution perspective. Remember: feelings are simply a warning sign. They are necessarily a good thing, even if the feelings themselves are negative. We should not ignore or repress our feelings, but instead should pay attention to them to figure out what information they give us about our needs. Needs, in turn, are simply the things we must get in order to feel comfortable again.

*Strategies*, then, are the *actions we take or behaviours we exhibit in order to meet our needs*. Defrosting a frozen pizza is one strategy to satisfy hunger; phoning in an order of Chinese food for delivery is another. Both are outward manifestations of an inner need to eat. Now consider the role of music itself. It's probably as vital a part of your life as breathing, and so you may be tempted to think of music as a need. But listening to, playing, or composing songs are all *behaviours* and *actions* (strategies). So what need does listening to, playing, or composing music fulfill? It may meet your needs for joy, creativity, self-expression, freedom, inspiration, companionship, mastery, or a host of other possible (and equally real) needs.

The problem is that strategies can run the gamut from the healthy and smart—like listening to, playing, or composing music—to the dysfunctional and destructive. Examples of the latter include everything from the passive (avoiding eye contact, remaining silent, refusing to participate), which meets our need to stay out of harm's way by avoiding conflict, to the more aggressive (arguing, name-calling, insulting, etc.), which might meet our need to win or to be right. Between these two opposites, there might be strategies we can call "passive-aggressive" (like insisting, "No, I'll be OK, move on," when clearly all observable signs, like the terse tone of voice and arms folded across the chest, suggest otherwise). Like the other strategies, these passive-aggressive approaches are intended, subconsciously at least, to deliver some sort of result and meet a need. Passive-aggressive behaviours may meet a need to feel righteous or to obtain some high moral ground ("Don't mind me, you look after yourself and I'll just suffer here quietly!") while simultaneously avoiding conflict.

Again, most of us aren't even aware that we are employing these strategies, because we've never been taught to decode them—neither our own nor others'. We usually accept them at face value. As with conflict resolution skills in general, most people have never learned how to "read" strategies and interpret them effectively. We seldom pause and reflect before interacting with each other in ways that are non-dysfunctional and non-destructive. Instead, we act instinctively and impulsively, using whatever strategies have worked for us in the past—however clumsy and unsophisticated they may be.

Babies offer a useful analogy here. Infants cry when they are tired, get stomach gas, or have dirty diapers, because they haven't yet developed language to express their need to sleep, be burped, or have their diapers changed. Babies are not conscious of using a strategy when they cry; at best they may be dimly aware of the feeling that provoked it. All they know is that they're uncomfortable and they need help to fix the problem. Crying seems to work, so naturally that's what they do.

Despite our greater mastery of language, adults aren't much different. Our feelings trigger the same old strategies because they seem to get us what we need. They're reliable, if blunt, instruments, and they've successfully kept us going as a species. Even though our brains are much better developed than our ancestors', our basic repertoire of responses has also become so hard-wired into our genetic programming that they've become automatic. Our ancestors' basic problem-solving approaches boiled down to some variation of fighting, fleeing, freezing, or fainting. In many ways, modern humans have evolved much beyond that, or so we like to think. But in truth our instinctive responses, actions, and behaviours often resemble fighting, fleeing, freezing up, or playing dead (fainting). If we feel a need to be validated, we will argue our viewpoint until we are acknowledged as being right (and will continue to argue as long as the desired response doesn't happen – indefinitely if necessary). If we feel a need to belong to the tribe, we will clam up or run away to avoid being ostracized. If we feel a need to have our opinion heard, we will yell or slam doors until someone finally hears. Like babies, when we need something, we tend to just act out, using the first available strategy without immediately worrying about its negative consequences.

As in more primitive times, any threat to our physical well-being is met immediately with the old "4-F" response. But our emotions react just as quickly (and crudely) to any perceived threat to our *mental* or *emotional* well-being, too. This includes threats—real or imagined—to things like our self-concept or identity. So if one person reacts to another's performance in a way that shakes the player's self-image as a virtuoso musician (for example), that psychic attack can be felt just as powerfully as a real, physical one. Just as someone whose physical safety is threatened by an attack will fend it off or retaliate bodily, a person whose non-material needs are threatened will also respond defensively. The only real difference is the latter defensiveness is more likely to manifest in the form of words.

For the sake of illustration, let's revisit the case of the guitarist who shows up late to band practice. The vocalist's emotional VU meter is crossing the threshold because he feels that his own time isn't being valued or respected by the guitarist. The singer's strategy for meeting the need to feel valued and respected (a strategy which, like the feelings and the need, is also in obscure code) might be to fix the guitarist with a challenging glare and bark, "You're late!" To the singer's unconscious mind, such a heavy-handed response is an easy way to assert authority or dominance and thus gain the desired respect. The problem, of course, is that such an impromptu strategy is likely to be met with a commensurate defense—or more accurately (since this is an emotional rather than physical attack), *defensiveness*. Lather, rinse, repeat: a cycle of attack and counter-attack is initiated and before long the band has a full-blown internal conflict on its hands.

Tragically, for many now-defunct bands (and humanity in general), we seldom allow our larger, more advanced brains the time—mere milliseconds, really—to pause, decode our feelings, figure out what the unmet needs are, and simply *ask for what we need* in the calm, polite way we would normally expect modern *Homo sapiens* to be capable of. As Viktor Frankl once wrote, "Between stimulus and response there is a space. In that space is our power to choose our response." (And, as the late Lou Reed sang, "Between thought and expression lies a lifetime....") In that space, we can choose to *respond*—not *react*—in a more highly evolved, helpful way rather than in the instinctive fight-or-flight mode. Instead of barking an accusation at his bandmate and setting off a vicious cycle that might lead to the disintegration of the group, the vocalist from our example who (justifiably) needed to feel respected and valued could have simply engaged in productive dialogue about his needs with his guitarist. A calm and mutually respectful discussion would have been a much better choice, a much more effective response.

When we learn to talk with each other at the level of our needs, it's much easier for us to understand each other and develop more effective, successful strategies for satisfying them:

"I notice we've been starting rehearsals later these last couple of weeks while we wait for everyone to arrive. A thought that I have about that is everyone's time isn't valued equally, and I don't like how that feels. I really need to feel like my time is valued, so what I request is for everyone to show up on time."

"Wow, OK. I had no idea it was impacting you like that...."

The problem, though, is that most of us have only learned to interact with each other at the level of our *strategies*, letting our actions and behaviours do the talking instead. Most of our strategies are dysfunctional: I bark at you, you bark right back at me.

"You're late again!"

"Oh, yeah? Well, you're not the boss of me...."

If actions speak louder than words, but our behaviours are equally inelegant and inarticulate, it's no wonder we have conflict. Without the training to respond differently, we will continue to react in our instinctive, inappropriate ways. So if what someone is doing or saying sets off your feelings VU meter, you are likely to react accordingly and jump straight into strategies—just like the barking, glaring band member in the example above—in a ham-handed attempt to protect or satisfy needs that are being threatened or unmet, without even consciously recognizing what those needs are. When people react negatively to someone's strategies (i.e., actions/behaviour), they are doing so because those particular strategies are being perceived as threatening or somehow violating their own need(s).

Before moving on to other examples, we'll take a quick step back, because we've only analyzed and decoded half of the interaction. We know the feelings and needs of the singer. If actions and behaviours are the outward manifestation of an unmet need, then what about the strategies of the guitarist? What unmet need is being addressed by his actions and behaviours of showing up late? It's hard to say without being able to ask the right questions, of course, but in this hypothetical example it's possible that the guitarist's tardiness is his way to exert control. Perhaps the rehearsal time was set without his approval or input, or perhaps he was simply outvoted. Unconsciously, then, our guitarist might have decided that he would assert his need for a sense of control by leaving the house at his own discretion, and not when the band "dictated" he should leave. Or it could simply be that leaving the house late was a way to satisfy his need for more time spent doing something else at home. Either way, showing up late is itself the unintended result of an unconscious strategy.

It's extremely useful to be able to analyze and decode these interactions, so let's look at a few more examples that we can break down into the feelings, needs, and strategies experienced by the parties. Although most conflicts can be quite complex, especially when they begin to spill over and involve others, we've kept the examples fairly simple to illustrate these concepts:

*Scenario #1:* The group has been in pre-production rehearsal for months and is ready to hit the recording studio to cut their first album. Brad is anxious to get into the studio because he feels the rest of the group is getting bored and stale playing the same old songs over and over, and gigs will be easier to get if they have songs recorded and on sale. He has done a lot of work to research studios and prices and has presented the band with several choices he feels represent the best value for money. Valerie, the other co-founder and leader of the band, is very methodical and logical and likes to take her time making decisions. She doesn't like rushing into anything. Brad is frustrated that Valerie is holding things up, even though he has presented her and the rest of the band with a lot of valuable information. Valerie, for her part, is comfortable with continuing to rehearse the songs because they just get better and better, and sometimes the band comes up with creative new arrangements and different musical twists. Mostly, though, she's concerned that she doesn't have as much information as she needs to make an informed decision despite Brad's efforts. Recording an album still represents a significant expense, and she wants to invest wisely. She has started to avoid looking at Brad during rehearsals or engaging with him, and they seldom talk outside the rehearsal room, if at all. The tension between Valerie and Brad is getting so thick that the other band members are starting to find excuses not to show up to rehearsal.

If Valerie, Brad, and the band were to recognize each other's behaviours as calls for help, and then sit down and discuss the situation, here's what they might find:

*Table 2: Scenario #1 - strategies, feelings and needs*

| Person | Strategy(ies) employed | Possible feeling(s) | Possible unmet need(s) |
|---|---|---|---|
| Brad | Nagging, coaxing, cajoling, veiled threats | Frustration, anxiety, fear of band breaking up | Group security & togetherness; accomplishment or challenge |
| Valerie | Avoidance, silence | Uncertainty, stress, exhaustion | More information, confidence, certainty; financial security |
| Other members | Arriving late, goofing off, or "showboating" during rehearsal | Worry, fear for band's future, boredom | Stability, calmness, direction |

Note that the *Possible* Feelings and *Possible* Unmet Needs listed here are only best guesses as to what may be going on for each of the parties involved. It's impossible to say with certainty what these things really are until and unless everyone acknowledges their actual, underlying feelings and explicitly identifies their unmet needs. Even then, you will often find that people aren't sufficiently in touch with their feelings and needs to be able to name them. (You may be one of those people!) The most important thing is to remember that the strategies, however annoying or frustrating they may be, are just attempts to express a need.

*Scenario #2*: Jenna and Xiang are two violinists in the symphony orchestra. Jenna has seniority by virtue of having been there the longest, but with the arrival of a new conductor she is worried that she may not automatically earn the nod as Concert Master, a prestigious position within the symphony. Xiang, a former child prodigy who is just as highly accomplished and somewhat younger than Jenna, has been with the symphony for less than two seasons. At first, Jenna welcomed Xiang in a friendly and almost protective way, but things changed once Jenna started hearing the orchestra's marketing team talk about how it wanted to "sex up" the symphony's image to appeal to a new demographic; Jenna began to worry that it might mean Xiang (or at least someone younger than herself) would get the promotion before her. Their relationship became decidedly frosty when Xiang started to cozy up to the new conductor, with whom she had previously worked in her freshman season with another orchestra. Jenna heard whispers that Xiang was saying decidedly unflattering things about her to the conductor and to other players in the orchestra as well, at which point Jenna silently declared war and dropped all pretense of kindness towards Xiang.

Here's what this particular situation might involve:

*Table 3: Scenario #2 - strategies, feelings and needs*

| Person | Strategy(ies) employed | Possible feeling(s) | Possible unmet need(s) |
|---|---|---|---|
| **Jenna** | Hostile, "cold shoulder" treatment towards Xiang | Jealousy, insecurity | Acknowledgement, recognition, or security |
| **Xiang** | Complaining to third parties ("triangulating") | Confusion, sadness, loneliness | Understanding, friendship, or a sense of acceptance & belonging |

*Scenario #3*: Nick and Dex are bandmates and songwriting partners. Now that the group is building a large and loyal following, and they've started to put their recordings up on YouTube and other outlets where they might earn more serious revenues, record companies are also beginning to sniff around. In short, things are getting serious. Nick has a great ear, and a natural way with words and melodies but, without any formal musical training or background, doesn't read or write music. Dex, on the other hand, is a trained multi-instrumentalist who knows all the chords on guitar and keyboard, and can transcribe the ideas onto paper or translate charts for Nick. Despite his own abilities, Dex senses that his musical ideas are best complemented by Nick's flair for word-smithing and melodic sense to really take flight. Nick, too, suspects that without Dex to help refine his tunes and make better sense of his contributions, his songs would be less likely to find an audience. Both, however, also think that they contribute the majority of the creative value to each song they co-write, and both think that they could probably find another partner if necessary. That's becoming more of a possibility with discussions about songwriting credits breaking down. As the pressure on the band mounts, both start digging in their heels. The tension is taking a toll on their songwriting partnership and on the rest of the band, who are really "hired guns" to Nick and Dex's lead roles.

If the two partners could sit down and discuss the situation a little more calmly, this is what they might discover:

*Table 4: Scenario #3 - strategies, feelings and needs*

| Person | Strategy(ies) employed | Possible feeling(s) | Possible unmet need(s) |
|---|---|---|---|
| Nick | Arguing, threatening to leave the partnership; withholding his best song ideas & contributions | Pride, anger | Fairness, recognition of contributions |
| Dex | Sabotaging Nick's contributions by deliberately playing incorrect notes & chords; disparaging Nick's contributions | Pride, anger | Fairness, recognition of contributions |

What's interesting about this last case is that both parties may actually have similar feelings and the *exact same needs,* yet their strategies are entirely different. Rather than see themselves being in opposition to each other, people in conflict should stop to explore just how closely aligned they often really are.

## Summary

In this section, we examined how feelings in conflict situations act as an early warning system alerting us to unhealthy situations or perceived threats or challenges. We now know the meaning and purpose of a range of feelings relating to conflict: frustration, for example, is what we feel when a need isn't being met; anger is a subsequent but equally natural reaction that energizes us to fight for something that is important to us; and so forth.

Most of these feelings relate to real human needs in the midst of conflict. People need to feel valued, respected, heard, and many other things. This, of course, is helpful in order to understand our own motivations and feelings, but if we can gain insight into the needs of the other party in a conflict situation, it gives us tremendous leverage in finding creative ways to meet these basic needs without having to sacrifice or compromise our own needs at the same time.

The problem is that most of us remain unaware of these needs, and in conflict situations we usually choose strategies to help us meet those needs in an equally unconscious fashion. A strategy is simply an approach to a particular problem; most of our instinctive ones are effective but crude (useful in the short term, but more damaging in the long term). The logic goes something like this: "Something happened and it hurt me, therefore this must be some sort of attack, and therefore I must lash out. If I hurt you the way you hurt me, you are likely to stop hurting me." This logic self-perpetuates and leads to a downward spiral of aggression and attack.

One way to help keep things from deteriorating is to speak from our own experience, but in order to do that without lashing out, we need to know the difference between authentic feelings and blaming feelings. An authentic feeling statement is, "I feel hurt"; a blaming feeling statement is, "I feel like you hurt me." Clearly the latter is bound to sound more like an accusation to the other party, and we shouldn't be surprised if the other person dismisses, denies, or deflects it and counters with an accusation of their own.

Next in Part III, we'll explore ways to prevent conflicts from happening in the first place and how to manage and resolve them more effectively, without escalating them or having them devolve into open warfare.

# Part III—Essential Conflict Prevention and Resolution Skills

By the end of this section, you will be able to

- apply two Guiding Principles of conflict prevention and resolution.

- use a checklist to ensure you follow all Four Steps to Conflict Resolution:
    1. Do a Perception Check.
    2. Synchronize Intent and Impact.
    3. Use "I" Statements.
    4. Follow the 5-step Fifth House Creative Conversations Model.

## The Way to Conflict Resolution

By now you should have a better-than-average understanding of how feelings, needs, and strategies work (for better or worse) in conflict situations. Next you will learn the fundamentals of how to successfully navigate through a conflict situation. If you stick with the principles described here throughout the conversation(s) and follow the steps using the skills to the best of your ability, you greatly increase the likelihood of an outcome that will benefit both you and the other person(s) in the conflict.

Even so, it's hard to wipe out a lifetime of bad habits and replace them with good habits overnight, so there may be quite a bit of deprogramming and reprogramming that has to take place in order to do it well. That's OK; skills take time to develop. The important thing is to do your best and remember that people will almost always respond positively when they see, hear, and experience a sincere attempt to fix an uncomfortable situation. It's likely that if you are not happy about the situation, the other person isn't, either, so they will probably appreciate your initiative and welcome the opportunity to resolve the issue.

There are many excellent books, videos, courses, and other resources on how to work through a conflict, and if you have the inclination, time, and opportunity, we certainly recommend that you check them out in order to increase your knowledge and enhance your skills. Our goal here is to give you what we consider to be the absolute must-have basics. We're keeping it simple in the belief that the less "technique" you have to worry about, the sooner you'll get past the conflicts, build confidence, and increase your conflict management ability. After all, it's hard to finesse a musical phrase if you haven't mastered the rudiments of the instrument.

First, there are two Guiding Principles to be applied throughout any discussion aimed at conflict resolution. These Guiding Principles are fundamental to preventing or resolving conflict. If you keep these in mind, and observe them at all times during a difficult conversation or conflict situation, you will greatly increase your likelihood of a successful outcome:

1.   Avoid the Conflict Escalation Triggers.

2.   Use Active Listening.

Both of these are explained in the next section. Once you're familiar with these and have practised using them, it's time to step into conflict resolution. The Four Steps to Conflict Resolution are:

1.   Do a Perception Check.

2.   Synchronize Intent and Impact.

3.   Use "I" Statements.

4.   Follow the 5-Step Fifth House Creative Conversations Model.

Each of these will be covered in turn, beginning with the Perception Check on page 127. But first, let's examine our two Guiding Principles:

# Avoiding Conflict Escalation Triggers

Imagine a band whose members have different creative visions for an album concept. This difference is not going to automatically generate a conflict, just like having different political views, religions, or ethnic backgrounds doesn't necessarily mean you will have a problem. Differences exist everywhere we look and can often be used to generate greater musical creativity. In fact, research suggests that a healthy amount of debate, disagreement, and dialogue is necessary to coming up with the best possible outcomes, if it means all ideas are well-dissected, analyzed, and "battle-tested." Furthermore, those engaged in the discussion are more likely to support the outcomes, because they feel satisfied that it's the best, most robust solution. The trick, then, is to allow for the differences without letting them lead to a conflict. The good news is that this is possible, even likely, because it's entirely within the power and control of those involved.

The bad news is that there are very specific Triggers that can almost guarantee that these differences turn into conflicts if one or more individuals is tempted to pull them. However, if you know what these Triggers are, then you can prevent conflict from occurring by not allowing yourself to be triggered by them, and by not using them to provoke others.

The deliberate choice to avoid the Triggers, coupled with the basic communication skills (beginning with Active Listening described in the next section), will set you well on the road to having a productive conversation with a great outcome. To reiterate: *you can control the outcome of a difficult conversation by ensuring that you do not give in to the temptation to use the triggers.* Like responding thoughtfully versus reacting emotionally, it is a choice. Make that choice and you will be delighted and amazed with the results.

Let's now take a look at what these Triggers are and how conflict escalates when they are used. Understanding the Triggers means knowing what *not* to do.

**Trigger #1: Using the word "You," followed by blame, accusation, exaggeration, or insult when having a discussion about something on which you disagree.** In a disagreement, you might begin talking about some*thing*, but it becomes a conflict as soon as the word "you" is used, at which point the discussion becomes about some*one*. In other words, the focus of the conversation shifts from what is wrong with the relationship or the situation, to what is wrong with the other *person*. (This should sound familiar to you from Part I!) When people hear the word "You" at the start of a sentence, they are primed to expect that what follows next is invariably some sort of accusation, judgment, or other personal attack. For example: "This is your fault!" (blame), "You're being irresponsible!" (accusation), "You never listen to me!" (exaggeration), or, "You don't know what you're talking about!" (insult).

Imagine yourself on the receiving end of any of these statements. When attacked, it's normal and natural for a person to become defensive and then go on the counter-attack. As discussed with regard to feelings, needs, and strategies, this is as true of verbal assault as it is of the physical variety. As soon as someone feels under attack, the conflict escalates from a *disagreement* to what we would call *personalized conflict*—because it has become personal. The conflict is no longer about an issue that needs to be fixed; now it's about a person. The situation has just been made worse, and so there are hurt or angry feelings to deal with in addition to the original problem.

Let's look at a typical difficult conversation, one that is still focused on fixing the person or judging them as bad or wrong instead of fixing the problem. Notice what happens when the word "you" is used. In the following everyday situation, observe how quickly the conversation between John and Jane degenerates as soon the latter enters the room:

**John** (understandably upset): "You're late! Rehearsal was supposed to start twenty minutes ago."

**Jane** (defensive now, accused of holding up rehearsal): "It's not my fault. The bus was late." [Shifting of blame.]

**John** (increasingly frustrated, due to apparent lack of responsibility and failure to apologize): "So? You should have taken an earlier bus."

**Jane** (getting more upset at being ordered what to do): "Oh right, like you're perfect, John? You're acting like I work for you!" [Return accusation.]

...And so the downward spiral continues.

Bottom line: by all means, *attack the problem—together—but never attack the person.* When you are having a difficult conversation about something you disagree over, stay focused on the issue. Only use the word "You" to start a sentence if it is followed by something neutral, positive, or a compliment. This is a conscious choice you will have to make if you want to keep the situation under control and prevent it from getting worse.

A better way to handle the conversation would be to wait for a calmer, cooler moment to bring up the issue. By pouncing on Jane immediately when she enters the room—no doubt already feeling flustered, guilty, or expecting to be shamed—she isn't in the best head space to have a trouble-free conversation. At that time the best opening line would be some sort of neutral observation. For example:

**John** (after rehearsal): "That was a good session! Now, Jane, I'd like to take a minute talk with you about today's late start time to see how to prevent it happening in the future."

**Jane** (if she hasn't already apologized for tardiness): "Yeah, I'm sorry about that. The bus was late." [Still feeling uncomfortable and thus shifting blame.]

**John** (taking the blame-shift in stride as a normal way for Jane to discharge the unpleasant guilt feelings): "I appreciate your apology. I understand the bus was late. What can be done to make sure we can start on time from now on, in case the bus is late again?"

Notice that John avoids inflaming tension by, first of all, starting on a positive note, and then by avoiding blame or judgment. He also successfully avoids triggering Jane by speaking from his own perspective and acknowledging her apology. John also reiterates what Jane says, demonstrating that John was paying attention to Jane rather than preparing some sort of speech, attack, or other response. John then invites Jane into a problem-solving dialogue rather than unilaterally imposing a solution, which is bound to backfire. The entire time, John carefully avoids using the word "you" in a negative way, particularly at the start of a sentence. As soon as that happens, Jane will likely stop listening. But John avoided the Trigger, and she remained open to dialogue.

When stuck in a *personalized conflict*, what typically happens is that as the level of emotional stress increases, the parties take it up a notch by using Trigger Number Two.

**Trigger #2: Proliferating the issues.** This means starting off talking about something specific but suddenly adding another issue—generally something contentious—into the mix.

This commonly happens when one brings up a problem from the past or introduces an unrelated issue to the one under discussion. To borrow the previous example, if John and Jane were trying to address the issue of starting on time for band practices, Jane might proliferate the issues by saying something like, "Yeah, well, I heard from your previous singer that you always used to show up late for practices, too." While the counter-claim of lateness may appear related to the original problem, it isn't; it dredges up history. The comment is not focused on the immediate problem and, worse yet, it also involves gossip that may be unfounded. It certainly doesn't help the current situation. A common reaction to such a statement would be defensiveness, denial, explanations, angry retorts, or counter-attack by John.

Note that it could just as easily have been John putting another unrelated issue on the table. Imagine an exasperated John, trying to address the issue of starting band practices on time, suddenly adding, "You know what else I don't appreciate? You're always bringing your girlfriend to our practices. We're supposed to be working, not socializing!" With that he has just plopped another, unrelated issue into the conversation. Again, the situation is ripe for devolving into personalized conflict. Eventually, "an eye for an eye makes the whole world blind," as the saying goes...all because one person gives in to temptation and uses Trigger #2.

Proliferating the issues is a sure-fire way to escalate conflict. Most of us can probably relate to this scenario: an argument with someone that starts off being about something relatively benign turns to upset and yelling, and soon neither party can even remember how the whole thing started. How did you get to this point? Easily! A simple disagreement, with both parties trying to work it out in a reasonable way, transforms into *personalized conflict when* one uses the word "You." Then someone digs up the past or introduces unrelated issues, further escalating the situation into *destructive conflict,* so called because it's here that things really start to fall apart.

Unfortunately, there is one more trigger that is guaranteed to make things even worse than they already are.

**Trigger #3: Talking to others about what happens between you.** By "talking to others," we don't mean trying to get some help or coaching about how to repair the situation; that would be an acceptable, helpful form of side-conversation. Instead we mean essentially gossiping or seeking sympathy from someone other than the persons directly involved in the conflict.

Some call this "triangulating," because it introduces a third person into the drama. Others might call it "blabber-mouthing," "feeding the rumour mill," or "running to Mom and Dad." Another term is "forum shopping," when we keep turning to others until we finally obtain the desired sympathy and support. Whatever you prefer to call it, the problem is that the people in conflict start talking to *other* people *about* each other—instead of talking *with* or *to* each other. In doing so, the person using Trigger #3 is effectively making the choice to escalate a conflict that has already entered the personalized stage and has been pushed to the destructive stage. By taking it even further it has escalated to what we call *hostile conflict*.

You probably know from your own experience that the purpose of talking to outside parties about the conflict, and about the people involved in it, is generally to convince the third party that our point of view is right and justified. In telling the story to others, we usually portray ourselves as the innocent victim of an injustice or perhaps the avenging hero. In either case, according to the old fairy tale paradigm so familiar from childhood, if we are the hero or the victim then logically the other person must be cast as the villain. As the victim or hero, it's easier to feel righteous about a position or to attain some higher moral ground to be used as leverage in an argument. In telling these dramatic tales, we are trying to get others to choose sides in the conflict—preferably our side and not the other's.

When this happens, those people newly enrolled in the drama will then typically talk to more outsiders, and they in turn talk to others, and so on. (Consider how many people you've ever involved in your own dramas have actually respected your request, "Don't tell anyone else, but you'll never believe what X said/did....") Before long, all sorts of people get involved and all kinds of crazy misinformation, warped perspectives, and unfair judgments abound. What results is usually a big, ugly mess.

Not surprisingly, by the time conflict gets to the hostile stage, it becomes quite difficult to resolve without some sort of intervention. This is because more people are now involved in the original unresolved conflict, and this additional complexity creates group dynamics that are tricky to manage. And for many of those dragged into the conflict, the whole matter starts to become about saving face rather than about actual problem-solving and conflict resolution.

Let's go back to our previous scenario and see what happens when it escalates to the *hostile conflict* stage and additional characters are drawn into our original drama starring John and Jane:

**Chuck** (to John): "Wow, Jane is really ticked off at you. Did you really threaten to kick her out of the band for being late?"

**John** (stunned by the surprise comment, defensive at the veiled accusation of dictatorship and by the betrayal of confidence): "Where did you get that idea?"

**Chuck**: "Jane told me herself."

**John** (temper rising): "And you believe her?" [Thinks: "That drama queen! She's always pulling this shit...."]

**Chuck** (now defensive because John thinks he's gullible): "Don't blame me, I'm just telling you what I heard."

**John** (to Dave): "Can you believe Jane? She went crying to Chuck, trying to gang up on me."

With each additional conversation, and with each new person pulled into the conflict, more fuel is thrown onto the fire. Left unchecked, it can develop into *polarized conflict*, which is hostile conflict taken to a whole new level, where battle lines are clearly drawn and factions are formed. Communication breaks down and the parties to a conflict take sides. Polarized conflict can split bands or entire companies apart, and, in many of the examples given in the earlier section on the history of conflict in the music industry, you've read just a few of the most egregious examples.

This scenario paints a gloomy picture, but take heart: you have just learned the three most important things to avoid doing if you want to prevent conflict from escalating or keep it from starting in the first place. Refuse to use those triggers!

If you can successfully avoid being activated by them or using them yourself, you have an enormous amount of control over creating a positive outcome whenever you are faced with a difference or disagreement. Take a good look at the illustration in Figure 8 that shows how quickly and easily conflicts can escalate due to the use of Triggers, often unintentionally. Commit it to memory, and start using this knowledge today.

*Figure 8: Conflict Escalation Triggers*

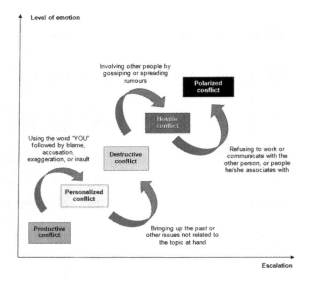

A key point to remember is that even while you consciously choose to avoid these Triggers, *it doesn't necessarily mean that the other person(s) in the conflict won't be using them.* Unless he or she has the same knowledge that you now have, it's possible—perhaps likely—that you will encounter these triggers in a conversation, particularly when the other person starts to feel nervous or uncomfortable. People use them all the time without even realizing it. When this happens, your job is to avoid taking the bait. Rise above it. Not everyone has the necessary conflict resolution skills, so you need to take the lead. Ignore at all costs any "You" statements directed your way, no matter how much they sting, otherwise you will find yourself triggered. Keep the conversation focused on the issue, the thing that needs to be fixed. Never retaliate.

You can help the other person in a disagreement reduce or eliminate their use of triggers by demonstrating how it's done. In setting a positive example, you can help them recognize their own button-pushing, whether it's deliberate or accidental. For example, you could say,

"Zoe, I just heard you say, 'You're always doing this.'* I'd prefer not to discuss the past right now. Let's stay focused on the present, which is how we are going to pay for the advertising we agreed to do. If you want, we can come back to your concerns about what it is that I'm always doing, if we can get the money issue dealt with first, OK?"

[*Note the Active Listening technique, addressed next in Part III.]

The next time someone tries to proliferate the issues, stay calm and focused. Recognize it for what it is, i.e., a covert strategy to satisfy some unmet need, however unclear it may be to you. For example, Zoe's frustration might be compounded if she thinks her barbed comment didn't have the desired effect. In this case she might then say something like, "Well, not only do we have a huge problem with how we're going to pay for the advertising, but you don't seem to realize that your songwriting is starting to suck—you haven't come up with anything really good for weeks now." As painful as that kind of comeback might be, resist the temptation to strike back. Your job is to lead the other person to a less confrontational, more satisfactory result.

Do this and *the outcome of this conversation is yours to control*. Since it's your choice what happens next, an appropriate response to Zoe's last shot would be something like, "OK, so we now have two things to work out: the money for the advertising and how the songwriting is going. Realistically, we can't talk about both things at the same time, so let's finish our conversation about the money. We'll see how long that takes and afterwards decide on when we should talk about the songwriting." In a way, successful conflict resolution is like fighting a fire: the best way to avoid a conflagration is to deprive it of more fuel.

It's worth repeating that unless you are in the enviable position of having a disagreement with someone of equal conflict resolution skills and knowledge, you will probably run into the Triggers. Refuse to be drawn in. Instead, make a conscious decision not to engage in any of the three Triggers yourself, even when they are being used against you. They almost certainly will be.

As discussed previously, without conflict resolution skills, people resort to the only reliable strategies they know will provoke a reaction (even if it's not the best, most productive kind of reaction). The use of Conflict Escalation Triggers is a covert, unsophisticated way of saying, "I feel guilty [etc.] and I'm really uncomfortable about this. I need you to truly understand what I am feeling right now, so I'll have to push your buttons until you feel as bad as I do, too!" Triggers almost always get the wrong kind of results, and unfortunately they're guaranteed to get attention—which is why people keep using them.

Rather than allow yourself to be hurt and risk retaliation, the best way to empathize is to simply acknowledge and validate the other person's pain. "Zoe," you might say, "I really get that you're upset by this. I'd probably be upset, too, in this situation." By exercising the choice to avoid Triggers yourself, you will always end up in a better position than if you had reacted to them. Afterwards, you can always go elsewhere and let off some steam, decompress, and shake it off, because preventing conflict from escalating is very hard work. It's good work, and necessary, but it is challenging and requires strength and stamina. Make sure you reward yourself for it.

# The Power of Active Listening

Regardless of where you are in a conflict scenario, whether you think something might be brewing or if you're already right in the thick of it, one thing is certain: *your single most powerful tool will be your ability to listen.*

Imagine a situation where you are in the early stages of a conflict. Perhaps you are upset with someone. You are worried, or suspicious, that they might have done something, or are about to do something, that would have a negative impact on you. So you muster up the courage to say something, because you really want to make sure everything is OK between you. You start telling them what's on your mind when they interrupt you. They take over the conversation with

- their version of the facts ("No, I don't think so, that's not how it how it went, this is what actually happened....")

- their denial of what you were saying ("No way, you can't seriously be thinking that—is this some kind of a joke...?")
- their feelings about what you were saying ("Hold on a second, I'm not OK with this, you are being totally disrespectful....")
- their dismissal of what you were saying ("How did you come to that conclusion? That's just ridiculous....")
- etc.

If that's the response to something you are trying to fix or figure out, chances are it doesn't feel good. If anything, you feel even worse than when you first broached the subject. You can probably appreciate what it's like not to be truly heard.

The reality is that few ever listen with full attention. Even at the best of times we devote only a few spare brain cycles to listening, never mind when we're in a conflict situation. Instead, if we really tuned in to our thought patterns, we'd notice that we're busy doing other things. There's a whole other inner conversation taking place! Mostly we're trying to "read between the lines" to find hidden meanings, interpreting (or misinterpreting) signals, and/or composing our response to what's being said. Instead of listening, we're really just waiting for our turn to talk. This is particularly true in conflict, when we're more likely to be reacting to Triggers and preparing justifications, rebuttals, or counter-attacks.

Now imagine that the individual you were trying to talk to kept quiet and listened to you. As you spoke, the only thing they said was, "Go on," or tried to make sure they understood what you were saying. They didn't add anything about themselves, didn't reality-check you (i.e., present an alternate interpretation of events or facts), and didn't give their opinion. They gave you all the time you needed to fully express yourself, and repeatedly checked in with you to make sure they were understanding you correctly. How would you feel then? Much better, of course.

Listening actively means turning off the interior chatter, offering occasional encouraging nods or sounds, and refraining from interruption. It also requires periodically reframing, restating, or rephrasing what is actually heard in order to check and demonstrate genuine understanding (as opposed to what is imagined or interpreted). Being able to accurately reflect back to the other person what they're saying proves to the other person that you are taking them seriously. It demonstrates to them that their perspective is important to you. It shows them that you truly care about what they think, and what they are experiencing.

Someone who feels that they are being taken seriously, that their perspective is important, and that they matter to you, will feel safe, at least on a subconscious level. They will feel respected regardless of whether or not you agree with them. And therein lies the power of active listening: if someone feels safe and respected, you can pretty much count on them to be willing to get through a difficult discussion and want a positive outcome as much as you do. Conversely, anyone who feels threatened, unheard, disrespected, or almost anything else will be more interested in defending, justifying, or attacking.

An active listener makes for a good role model. The other party can make the connection between how good it feels to be heard properly and how much better things go as a result. With a little luck and encouragement, they will try it, too. An otherwise vicious cycle can be turned into a virtuous circle of clearer communication and improved relationships. If you want to fix something with someone, it's wise to help them get into a head space where they will want to fix it with you, too. That way you ensure the best possible outcome for yourself, for them, and for the situation. Of all the strategies to employ in a conflict situation—consciously or unconsciously – active listening is by far the best.

## Why is Listening so Difficult?

As much as it makes sense to utilize the power of listening, the truth of the matter is that listening—truly *hearing*—is difficult. There are many reasons for this, all of them legitimate. Here are just a few:

1. *We think at 400-500 words per minute but speak at 125-150 words per minute.* This means that in the sixty seconds it took Scott to say only a couple of sentences, Jason's mind—his thought process—is already racing way ahead, simply because that part of our brain works that much faster. By the time Scott got his first two sentences out, Jason has already begun to:

   - *interpret* ("OK, so Scott's really mad about us deciding to change guitarists. He's trying to keep his cool but I can tell he's peeved....")
   - *decode* ("Well, I don't know what his problem is. Jeff isn't the greatest live guitarist, we all know that. I think it's because Scott and Jeff are good friends, so that's probably the real reason why he's upset....")
   - *judge* ("Scott just needs to face up to the fact that it didn't work out with Jeff. There's a big difference between live and studio playing, and Scott needs to man up and call it like it is. If we're going to be successful we're all going to have to make tough decisions sometimes. Not sure Scott is cut out for that....")
   - *evaluate* ("I can kind of see his point of view, but on the other hand he doesn't have anything to complain about. We gave Jeff a chance, we decided that we'd see how things worked out because he doesn't have a lot of experience playing live. And as it turns out he just doesn't cut it....").

2. *We are susceptible to distractions.* There is an endless supply of distractions—in fact we are constantly bombarded with them. Listening demands that we focus on the speaker and on what he or she is saying, and it means that we aren't doing anything but that. The only exceptions are the small interjections that we might offer in order to demonstrate attention, encourage the speaker, and show understanding of what is being said ("I

see," "Yes," "Go on," etc.). A partial list of common distractions would include:

- incoming texts, phone calls, or social media messages
- any other current issues or concerns (relationships, work, school, etc.), whether related or unrelated to this one
- physical sensations (being hungry, feeling tired, medical issues, hangovers, etc.)
- visual distractions (TV, people, animals, scenery, etc.)
- body language, including facial expressions
- background noise
- etc.

3. *We have expectations and assumptions.* If we go into a difficult conversation already expecting the other person to receive us in a certain way, act a certain way, or say certain things, we will be looking to confirm those expectations. We'll observe how they speak and behave and interpret it so that it lines up with our predictions. It's human nature to check that anything we see or hear provides evidence that what we anticipated is correct. Psychological literature calls this common problem "confirmation bias." In other words, we are predisposed to seeing patterns that prove us right—even if those patterns aren't actually there. It may comfort you to know that this well-studied phenomenon doesn't just happen to people in conflict, it can happen to everyone in all kinds of situations... including scientists working alone on their research. We tune in to those frequencies, figuratively speaking, and tune everything else out. This means we are not truly listening but are selectively filtering out the information that doesn't fit with our mental image or expectations.

Expectations are dangerous because they can easily turn into self-fulfilling prophesy. For instance, let's say that a band meeting has been called by Janice, who is the band's founder. Tom, who has been experiencing some friction with Janice lately, figures that he will either be sacked or at least have the riot act read to him by Janice. As he makes his way to the practice room, he is having a different kind of rehearsal in his head: fuelled by his expectations, Tom is preparing arguments to use against Janice and is thinking about venting all his pent-up feelings and frustrations. With every step, he is working himself into a state of righteous anger. By the time he reaches the studio, he's primed to explode at the slightest trigger, however inadvertent.

But for all he knows, Janice may simply want to try out her new-found conflict resolution skills, perhaps discuss changing the set list, or maybe make an announcement that has nothing to do with Tom. Because he anticipated the worst, when he walks in with a scowl and the other band members greet him, he hears everything as either sarcasm, pity, or condescension. If someone asks, "What's wrong?" out of genuine interest, Tom responds with unnecessarily cutting comments and pretty soon the situation devolves from a potentially happy outcome into a loud, sustained argument, culminating in Tom's impromptu firing.

"See?" he exclaims. "I knew all along that you guys just wanted me out of the band."

Tom gets to be right about his expectations—but he's far from happy about it. To avoid this outcome, always check your own expectations and, when necessary, ask yourself: would I rather be *right* or *happy*? Remain open to being pleasantly surprised.

We often go into difficult conversations assuming we know all the facts, have all the information, or know what the other person is about—we've already "figured them out." Assumptions in this situation act much like expectations: we are waiting to observe or hear things from the other person that only serve to validate our assumptions. Anything that doesn't agree with our assumptions gets filtered out, and thus a lot of opportunity for true understanding is lost.

For example, Robin might notice that Dan is withdrawn and uncommunicative in rehearsal. There are all kinds of things Robin might assume from Dan's behaviour: Dan is mad. Dan is bored and wants to quit. Dan doesn't care. But in truth Dan might have received some bad news from home shortly before showing up to rehearsal. Maybe Dan is having money troubles, or he split up with his girlfriend.

Robin could simply ask Dan what's wrong and why he's not his usual, engaged self. But if this were a conflict situation, it wouldn't be so simple. We commonly attribute other people's behaviours to motivations that simply aren't necessarily true. The reasons seem plausible to us because that's how we might behave ourselves if we were feeling the way we perceive the other person to be feeling, based on their behaviour. In a conflict, an unanswered phone message, text, or email could be taken as a sign that the other person is angry or doesn't care—although it could just as easily mean that their smart phone battery ran out of power. If Dan suddenly snapped at Robin, Robin might attribute that to something she had said or done to offend Dan. But it's just as likely that seconds earlier Dan was thinking about his empty bank account or the fight with his girlfriend. If Robin automatically assumes that it's directed towards her—which she's likely to do if there's already some tension between them—then responding in kind will just escalate the situation. Always test assumptions, beginning with your own.

4. *Active listening is a skill that must be learned and is seldom innate.* While some people are uncannily good listeners, we generally have to learn the skills to listen actively.

Another thing that often makes listening surprisingly difficult is one to which every musician reading this book can relate: we think that we're naturally adept at listening just because we're born with ears that never shut off even while sleeping. Don't conflate hearing with listening! *Active* listening requires a particular set of abilities, just as becoming proficient on any instrument takes constant practice, application, and refinement of techniques. It's not enough to learn where the notes are on the scale; you have to repeat them over and over in order for your movement to become sufficiently fluid. Even then, you have to try different fingerings to hear the best result. Much of it is trial-and-error. And the only real way to judge how adept you've become is to play an entire composition, in context, and not just repeat scales or chord progressions *ad infinitum.*

Listening is just like that. Some of us may have a more natural talent for it than others, but either way, we only get good at it by developing the skills and using them regularly. Only a certain percentage of musicians ever become professionals; likewise, only a relatively small number of us ever become sufficiently skilled at truly listening. The difference is that *everyone* can become a good active listener, with practice.

5.    *We believe it is more important to speak than to listen.* This should come as no surprise for most of us, because this is how we've been programmed since childhood.

As youngsters we are often not taught conflict resolution skills by our parents or caregivers. Conflict is typically handled through some sort of disciplinary measure, such as time-outs, punishment, and so forth. The voice of authority puts an end to any argument. When we enter grade school, conflict resolution skills are not typically part of the curriculum, either. Once again, conflict between students is typically dealt with by authority figures meting out consequences, as opposed to some form of genuine resolution. By the time we get to high school, we experience more of the same: conflict resolution skills are not part of the curriculum, and it's usually managed by authority figures and with consequences. Things do shift a bit in high school, though: often we find that conflict goes underground and is dealt with in surreptitious ways. It might take the form of bullying, shunning, or harassment. It's typically about getting the last word or being the loudest.

Sadder still, once we enter the workforce, we find that the adult approach to conflict isn't much different. Now the authority figure is the boss, and the consequences are typically fear of reprisal or job loss. It is still relatively rare for employers to ensure that employees receive training in conflict resolution skills in the workplace, even though it's very much in their interest to do so. But why should work communications be any different from the rest of our public interactions?

Even our democratically elected governments, which we think of as the hallmarks of a civilized society, do more talking than listening. Political debates are the primary method of dealing with differences in ideologies. Just like school, our houses of government celebrate or reward argument and rhetorical abilities far more than skills of genuine dialogue. All things considered, the fact that most people don't have conflict resolution skills is not a reflection of who they are as human beings but rather a reflection of what society values.

6.  *We are preparing our commentary or rebuttal.* Due to the same programming, when in conflict we automatically default to the "I'm right, so you must be wrong" setting. This basically ensures that when we stop speaking, we rarely actually listen to our counterpart, but instead prepare our rebuttal. (Seeing the other party as an opponent instead of a *partner* in solving our mutual problem is another major obstacle to listening.) If we happen to be in agreement, we are typically preparing to comment on that point of accord. As such, we are not actually listening to understand; we are really listening to highlight what we disagree or agree on.

Clearly, then, listening is not easy. Real listening takes effort, and some of that work includes reprogramming and learning new skills. However, in doing so we equip ourselves with what is probably the most powerful ability in human interaction. You can imagine how hard it would be to stay angry and remain in conflict with someone who is clearly doing their best to listen, genuinely understand you, and make room for your point of view. Listening is very seductive and disarming, and will almost always put you in a position that will greatly increase the possibility of a successful outcome to a difficult situation.

# How to Demonstrate We Are Listening: Essential Listening Skills

Active Listening is the second Guiding Principle of conflict resolution. As with the first principle (staying away from the Conflict Escalation Triggers), it's critical to exercise the principle of Active Listening from beginning to end in any difficult or conflict situation. Make a commitment to listen to the best of your ability any time you are trying to prevent a conflict or resolve one. You will have to prove to the other person(s) that you are listening to them for two key reasons. First, they need to know you are being sincere and want to have a genuine dialogue with them. If they suspect you just want to keep scoring points, they won't listen, either. Second, it's an effective strategy for giving them what they might need to feel safe and comfortable, and to help reduce the level of stress and anxiety in the conversation.

Note that active listening doesn't necessarily mean you have to *like* the person you're dealing with. And while you won't always be able to achieve agreement, you need at least to be able to understand each other's perspectives. If you're going to work with them on any musical level, you can't afford to have conflict get in the way. Prove to them that you are listening. This is done by using three basic active listening skills:

1. Paraphrasing
2. Summarizing
3. Empathic responses

**Paraphrasing**: Paraphrasing is repeating back to the speaker what you have just understood them to say, but *in your own words*. You do not repeat back to them the exact words of what they just said, which is parroting and can easily be seen as mockery or sarcasm. Instead, paraphrasing proves to the speaker that you have been listening because they are hearing a very close version of what they have just expressed. Subconsciously they will conclude that you must be listening, otherwise you wouldn't be able to accurately interpret what they just said. Thus, paraphrasing validates for the speaker that you are taking them seriously and not just selectively hearing what you want to hear (i.e., fulfilling your expectations) or twisting their words to fit your own agenda.

It's good practice to wait until they have made their point before you begin. Never interrupt, or it will just lead to more frustration. Sometimes it's useful to start your paraphrasing with, "What I heard you say was...," or, "What I understood from what you said was...," or similar wording. It signals your desire to check your understanding of their point of view rather than just reinforcing or reframing your own.

For example, let's say John is upset that Jane is late for rehearsal again. The conversation might go thus:

**John**: "I really hate it when you're late because the rest of us are always here on time. We have to make sure we leave our homes and jobs in enough time to get here by band practice, but for some reason you don't do that, and it makes me feel like you don't care about us as much as you care about yourself and the stuff you have to do."

**Jane**: "What I heard you say is that you are upset that I don't value your time because you make more of an effort to arrive on time, whereas I don't."

**John**: "Yeah, I guess that's what I'm saying."

Notice that Jane wisely ignores the hyperbolic use of "always" (and its implication that Jane is "never" or "seldom" on time). Instead, Jane focuses in on the real underlying truth of what's being said by John. She restates the core elements of what John is saying but *in her own words*. It's not exactly what John said verbatim, but it's a close approximation—minus some of the more inflammatory rhetoric.

If you happen to misunderstand what is said or misrepresent what is intended, paraphrasing allows the opportunity for the other person to clarify or correct before any further miscommunication develops. It's human nature to want to be understood, and the other person will not hesitate to amend a paraphrase or restatement that is not in line with what they said. For conflict to be resolved there needs to be good understanding and clarity between you as you work through a conflict.

It's possible that when they hear you paraphrase they will realize that what they said is not really what they meant, or maybe your paraphrase wasn't entirely accurate. Either way, simply restate what you hear them saying as they reframe or clarify their original statement(s). Keep doing this from a place of genuine curiosity until they're satisfied that you truly get what they're saying. It won't work if all you're doing is deliberately misquoting them in order to make them look bad or feel guilty! The goal is comprehension. There's no question that it requires patience and practice, but, once again, paraphrasing enables deeper understating between individuals.

Let's take a second look at the example, but this time let's say that for some reason Jane doesn't quite nail the paraphrasing the first (or even second) time. Maybe Jane focuses on the wrong thing, or allows emotions to get in the way and finds it hard to resist the temptation to be defensive. The same conversation might go something like this:

**John**: "I really hate it when you're late because the rest of us are always here on time. We have to make sure we leave our homes and jobs in enough time to get here by band practice, but for some reason you don't do that, and it makes me feel like you don't care about us as much as you care about your own time and the stuff you have to do."

**Jane**: "What I heard you say is that you have concerns because you're always here on time and I'm not."

**John**: "No, that's not what I meant. Look, we all have stuff outside of band practice we have to do, but at least we're making efforts to get here on time, and you don't seem to have the same commitment."

**Jane**: "What I understood you to say was that you don't believe I have the same commitment to the band."

**John**: "No, that's not it either. I think you're committed to the band, but you don't operate on the same schedule as the rest of us and it pisses me off."

**Jane**: "Ah, OK. What I get out of what you just said is that when I show up late you feel I don't value your time as much as I value my own."

**John**: "Yes! That's it."

See how much better that turned out?

**Summarizing**: Summarizing is the skill of helping to make a person's point for them. Sometimes, when people are really worked up, they lose some ability to be articulate; it's hard for them to choose just the right words to express themselves. Perhaps they're angry and their brain is overwhelmed with adrenaline, they're hyperventilating and not getting enough oxygen, or they may be so energized that they carry on for a while. Either way, to summarize effectively, you simply listen through everything that they are saying and then, in your own words, feed back to them what you understand to be the gist of what they are saying.

Summarizing is typically used when too much has been said to properly paraphrase, usually because the speaker is venting. When people vent, they are often just repeating one or two main themes. Summarizing what they are saying, as with paraphrasing, is validating; the person who is upset will feel that they've been heard and taken seriously. This will help them to move forward in the conversation. Again, summarizing accurately proves that you are listening to them, and this can only help.

Let's look at another scenario to demonstrate the skill of summarizing:

**Mick**: "I don't see why you should get 50% credit for writing this song when I came up with most of the melody for the verses and the chord structure. You just came up with the chorus melody, a bass line, and suggested changes to the bridge. Maybe changed a few notes of the verse. You always want to split credit and money equally but you don't split the work equally—you show up late for loading the gear into the van for gigs, you didn't help us find the new rehearsal space, you don't do as much as the rest of us when it comes to looking for gigs or doing promotion! Last gig you said you were sick and didn't help put up posters around town, but the rest of us had bad colds, too, and we still went out postering! I don't see why you deserve the same credit. Maybe you started the band and it's your band name, but the rest of us do a lot of the heavy lifting, too! You don't automatically get the same credit."

**Keith**: "What I understood you to say was that you don't think that I contribute equally to group work."

**Mick**: "Yes, I guess that's what I am saying."

The magic of paraphrasing and summarizing is that when the other party feels like they've been heard and understood they feel less of a need to keep making their point, which in turn reduces your need to make counter-points, and so on.

**Empathic responses**: Of all the listening skills, empathy is probably the most powerful. It is similar to paraphrasing or summarizing, except that instead of reflecting back to the speaker the *content* of what they have said, you are reflecting back the *feeling* behind what they are saying. The focus is taken off the words and is instead shifted to the emotional content.

Empathic responses take listening to a deeper level, and thus provide even stronger proof that you are really hearing the speaker. This is because you have to go beyond interpreting what the speaker is saying—that is, the external or surface story—into the inner, unseen emotional territory. A skillful empathic response demonstrates to the speaker that not only do you understand what they are saying, but you also understand what they are feeling. As mentioned before, try to imagine staying in battle mode with someone who is clearly demonstrating that they care enough to not only get what you are saying, but also get what you are feeling. Here we should stress that *understanding* someone does not necessarily mean that you *agree* with them! Strategically speaking, however, if you want to get somewhere in a conflict, you will go a lot further and a lot faster if the other person feels heard and understood.

Let's revisit our previous examples. This time instead of paraphrasing or summarizing, we'll show how the conversations might sound when empathic responses are used:

**John**: "I really hate it when you're late because the rest of us are always here on time. We have to make sure we leave our homes and jobs in enough time to get here for when rehearsal starts, but for some reason you don't do that, and it makes me feel like you don't care about us as much as you care about your own time and the stuff you have to do."

**Jane**: "So this has all become really frustrating for you."

**John**: "Well DUH. Wouldn't you be frustrated?"

**Jane**: "You bet I would be."

If the other party in the conflict is reassured that you "get" them, emotionally speaking, then once again they won't have to try as hard to make you feel their pain—literally or figuratively.

Here's our second example, this time using empathic responses to connect:

**Mick**: "I don't see why you should get 50% credit for writing this song when I came up with most of the melody for the verses and the chord structure. You just came up with the chorus melody, a bass line, and suggested changes to the bridge. Maybe a changed a few notes of the verse."

**Keith**: "So you're thinking this is not a fair situation for you."

**Mick**: "Oh, yeah? Well how's this for not fair: you always want to split credit and money equally but you don't split the work equally—you show up late for loading the gear into the van for gigs, you didn't help us find the new rehearsal space, you don't do as much as the rest of us when it comes to looking for gigs or doing promotion!"

**Keith**: "The way things are going have been really disappointing for you."

**Mick**: "Last gig you said you were sick and didn't help put up posters around town, but the rest of us had bad colds, too, and we still went out postering! I don't see why you deserve the same credit. Maybe you started the band and it's your band name, but the rest of us do a lot of the heavy lifting, too! You don't automatically get the same credit."

**Keith**: "There's a bunch of things that are really upsetting for you about all of that."

Again, although it's frequently hard to find the right words in the midst of the emotional turmoil of conflict, it's worth the practice and the effort. Resisting temptation to rebut, argue, or interject with your own feelings is also difficult. If you must assert your own point of view in a discussion, the best thing you can do is be mindful of your framing and language; subtle signals can be powerful.

We recommend that you get into the habit of replacing the word "but" with "and." This slight change of phrase signals the possibility that both points of view may be valid, and both can co-exist peacefully. Notice the difference between these two statements:

a. "I understand you think the bridge should go here, but I think it should come later, after the second verse."

The word "but" here effectively dismisses everything that precedes it. In other words, the second part of the sentence—the speaker's opinion—basically invalidates or overrides the first. In this sense the speaker is elevating his opinion over the other person's. The fact that the speaker thinks one thing negates the other's opinion on the matter.

b. "I understand you think the bridge should go here, and I

## UNHELPFUL COMMUNICATION

**Warning!** The following are examples of unhelpful communication. They have no place in the business of listening and will only serve to derail your efforts at resolving conflict:

- Criticizing
- Sarcasm
- Name-calling
- Unsolicited advice
- Ordering
- Threatening
- Mind-reading
- Exaggeration
- Interrupting
- Minimizing
- Reassuring (can easily be interpreted as patronizing)
- "Technique-ing" without sincerity (i.e., using conflict resolution knowledge as leverage)
- Focusing only on facts and disregarding feelings involved, or vice versa
- Clichés, etc.
- Monopolizing the conversation
- Changing the topic
- Etc.

think it should come later after the second verse."

Notice in the second sentence the word "and" indicates that there are two truths—the speaker's and the other person's—and neither is lessened or overruled by the other. All it really does is juxtapose the two points of view without privileging one over the other. It invites the possibility that both perspectives are valid.

# Preventing or addressing conflict in its early stages

There are four steps to conflict resolution (remember to use the two Guiding Principles of conflict resolution, described above, throughout):

1. Do a Perception Check.

2. Synchronize Intent and Impact.

3. Use "I" Statements.

4. Follow the 5-Step Fifth House Creative Conversations Model.

Let's examine these four steps in detail, keeping in mind that whenever you want to resolve a conflict, you should follow *all four steps in this order*—don't skip any, and don't switch them around. This will increase your chances of a successful outcome.

## Step One: Do a Perception Check

Before attempting any conflict resolution work, check and make sure that what you *think* is going on is actually happening. Humans, being who and what we are, tend to perceive a situation according to our mental models of how the world works. We might believe, for example, that someone who raises their voice does so only because they're angry, when it might simply mean they have a blocked ear and can't hear themselves very well. We often employ these "perceptual filters" to screen out information that doesn't conveniently match our stories or expectations.

It's all too common to be unduly affected by events or actions when they're seen through the lens of prior experience. For example, a band member might have been excluded from the decision-making process in a previous group and so he may fear a recurrence of that situation. If the same band member isn't consulted on a particular decision, no matter how trivial, he might see it as a sign of trouble when it really might have just been a matter of convenience and timeliness.

It's important to remember that these perceptions or impacts actually tend to be more about us and our interpretations than about something that the other party in the conflict has actually said or done. In other words, before sitting down with the other party (or parties) to iron out a perceived conflict, make sure there is really an issue. In some cases you will be pleasantly surprised to learn that it was all a simple misunderstanding.

Checking your perceptions is therefore the first vital step in successful conflict resolution—and sometimes it can also be the last one. When we check our perceptions, it is quite possible there is actually no problem at all. ("I'm not mad at you at all! I just got into a near-accident on the way to rehearsal, and I'm still shaking.") So before launching into the hard work of listening and exercising your conflict resolution skills, just make sure all of that energy and effort is warranted. This reality-testing is known as a Perception Check.

There are three sub-steps to a Perception Check:
a. Describe what you are noticing.
b. Ask what it means.
c. Turn judgment into curiosity.

***First: Describe what you are noticing.*** At this stage, something has happened or something was said that doesn't sit well with you. The emotional VU meter is trembling. Rather than sweeping it under the rug, hoping it will go away, and risking a buildup of resentment, you go into conflict prevention mode and address what is bothering you. What was it, exactly, that was said or done that troubles you? Without attaching any interpretation at all, describe the situation to your-self (remember to stay away from the Triggers!). Describe the *it*—the *what*—and not the *who*. Write it down. Avoid any inflammatory or judgmental words. Don't use any of the unhelpful communication methods, like exaggerating, minimizing or criticizing. (See the side-bar under *The Five Steps of a Fifth House Creative Conversation Model* for more information on unhelpful communication.) Using neutral words, describe what was said or what happened in such a way that any bystander would agree is factually accurate.

You could say, for example, "I noticed that a decision has been made as to the order of the songs on the album." This is a far more factual, objective, and helpful description of the situation than, "What the hell is going on here? Did you guys deliberately not let me have any input on the running order?!"

The latter may be an accurate reflection of your inner state—your thoughts and feelings—and in that sense is subjectively "true," but it can't be independently verified by a casual observer. The inflammatory language, accusations, etc., are probably evidence of how you feel, but they don't actually describe the situation itself. The idea here is to cap-ture the *words, actions, and other visible, external artifacts of the situation*. Internal things like feelings and judgments or thoughts aren't helpful in this instance. (You'll address feelings and needs eventually.) Clearly the neutral observation will set the conversation off on a much better footing than the personalized interpretation.

A conversation that starts neutrally invites a response equally free of negative vibes, for example, "I realize it may look that way, and we haven't actually decided anything. We were just trying to visualize how the album cover might look with the track listing in place."

Perhaps just by doing the very first part of a Perception Check—describing what you are noticing—it will clear the air and prevent a conflict. The other party now understands that you might be upset be-cause of how you perceived something, and they can help clarify the situation. There's no longer an issue.

On the other hand, starting off with an interpretation—especially one that turns out to be incorrect—is much more likely to provoke a defensive reaction along the lines of, "Hey chill out! You got it all wrong—how could you even think that of us!?" Before the conversation started, only one party was upset; now there's two. It was an unnecessary conversation that started and ended badly, when it really didn't need to take place at all.

Let's assume your perception-check was greeted with something like, "Yes, that's right, we discussed the running order at the pub last night after practice." In other words, what if your perception seems to be correct, and there may be a conflict here? Then you would move on to the second part of a Perception Check:

***Ask what this additional set of facts means.*** Following the same example, you would say something like this: "Oh, okay, tell me how that came about." This response leaves room for a possible answer like this one: "None of us really wanted to do it without you, but we got a call from the guy who's writing a review on his blog and he said that he needed to know the running order so he could post it immediately."

Again, you might not like the answer but at least now you know what happened and why, so you leave room for the possibility that it was nothing personal. There was no conspiracy against you, nor was there a deliberate attempt to undermine your voting power in the band. These types of thoughts are really judgments: *they were wrong* to do what they did; *they don't care* about my feelings; *my vote doesn't count*; and so on. That being the case, you can now move to the third part of a Perception Check:

***Turn judgment into curiosity.*** This sub-step means stop evaluating and instead gather more information. Continuing with our example, you can engage your curiosity about the situation and say something like this: "Do you guys know what changed for the blogger? I understood he was doing the review next week." With this response, you open up a dialogue about what actually happened (as opposed to your thoughts, judgments, or perception of what happened) and you can discuss the real issue, which is how you came to not be involved in the decision-making about the running order.

The goal here is not to find fault or point fingers (who did what to whom and why); it's simply to account for the sequence of events. Contrast this response with a judgment that might sound like this: "Well, you should have told him that we can't just accommodate his schedule any time he wants to change something!" Again, a response like this—effectively an accusation (i.e., "You failed to do something!")—would typically put the other person into defensive mode, with the band members involved rapidly careening towards a conflict. It's easy to get confrontational with someone who starts flinging accusations, but it's a lot harder to get mad at someone who's simply seeking to satisfy his or her curiosity.

To summarize, a Perception Check is always the first step towards conflict resolution. In the best-case scenario, when doing a Perception Check you may discover that there isn't actually a problem; in the worst-case scenario, you will get clear on what the issue is so that you can work towards resolving what *actually* needs to be fixed, as opposed to what you might *imagine* needs to be fixed. If after doing a Perception Check you determine that there really is something that needs to be dealt with, you will then move to the second step, which is to *Synchronize Intent and Impact*.

## Step Two: Synchronize Intent and Impact

If after your Perception Check you determine that there really is an issue that needs to be addressed, your next step is to set your intention so that you maximize the positive impact that you seek. In other words, the second step after the Perception Check is to get clear on your reason(s) for having the conversation so that it has the desired effect—namely, to clear the air, resolve the issue, and move forward with the relationship intact. This is critical because you want to be able to start the conversation on a positive footing. You want to make sure that the other person knows why you are raising the subject—you don't want them to have to guess at anything, because they could guess incorrectly. If the intention behind the conversation isn't clear and positive, there's a good chance it will be poorly received; the impact will be negative. Transparency is key.

Checking in with yourself first is also a crucial step, because you need to make sure you have the "right" motivations for having the conversation with the other person, i.e. the intention to prevent or resolve conflict. It's not about proving yourself right, making the other person wrong, and/or having the last word. The intent should never be to make them feel as bad as you do about the situation.

As with the Perception Check, you should write down your purpose for having the conversation with the other person. Be honest. At the same time, make sure that you set an intention that is honourable, i.e. one that is ultimately about repairing or strengthening the relationship. You might truly feel the need to convince the other person of your point of view because you think you are misunderstood, but continuing to argue your case would only make matters worse. Here are some examples of setting positive intentions and their intended impacts:

- "My intention is to understand what is going on between us so that we can get along better." (Not, "My intention is to let her know that I am fed up about how things are going between us, and if it doesn't stop, I am out.")

- "My intention is to talk about how decisions are made so that I feel more comfortable." (Not, "My intention is to put my foot down about the band's decision making and insist that we have a democratic process.")

- "My intention is to express how I feel about how the auditions are going so that I can get it off my chest and feel heard." (Not, "My intention is to tell him that the auditions are wasting everybody's time and he needs to wake up and smell the coffee.")

The point of setting our intention is to get clear about *what* needs to be discussed (not *who*), in order to make sure that the resulting impact will be a positive one. It's worth reiterating that unless we clarify our intentions from the outset, *people will infer our intention based on how they are being impacted by what we are saying.* Quite simply, if what we say lands in such a way that they feel bad, they may assume that our intention was to hurt them. Conversely, *we assume that what we say will be received in the spirit in which it is intended,* which is not always the case. This is why it's always critical to synchronize the *intent* of the conversation with its desired *impact*, and both need to be positive and constructive.

When it comes to conflict prevention and resolution, there is very little room for assumptions. Incorrect ones only make a situation more difficult in the end. It is all too common for conflict to have its origins in the dynamics between intent and impact, because it is alarmingly easy to incorrectly attribute motivations or misread the purpose behind someone's words or actions. Flare-ups can occur just because one party inadvertently utters the wrong word, and the other party assumes it was deliberately chosen to wound. As soon as there has been a disconnect between intentions and the resulting impact, the miscommunication continues.

Once the Perception Check is done, you have verified that there is indeed a situation that needs to be addressed, and you have set your intention in a way that will create the positive impact you desire, it's time to start talking to the other person. You are now ready to move to the third step in conflict resolution, and the best way to approach this is through the use of "I" Statements.

## Step Three: Use "I" Statements

The "I" Statement is so called not because there is anything particularly selfish or self-centred about it, but because you are *speaking from your personal experience or point of view only.* "I" Statements are a way to ensure there is never any blame, motivation, or fault attributed to the other person during the conversation, even accidentally. That's because when a sentence contains (and especially begins with) the word "You," the listener assumes that what is about to follow is inevitably some sort of accusation or attribution, i.e., "You said this," or, "You did that." Such expectations invariably shut down the listening process and provoke defensiveness. On hearing the trigger word "You," the listener prepares to ward off an imminent attack and is no longer prepared to engage in productive dialogue. Speaking in "I" Statements ensures that you refer only to yourself, your perceptions, your feelings, and your interpretations only. It's a good way to demonstrate that you're taking responsibility for your own contributions to the situation.

The basic formula for an "I" Statement is as follows, and it is adaptable to any situation:

---

**I am/feel** _____
     (Describe feeling)

**About/When** _____, and
          (Describe issue)

**I would appreciate it if** _____
               (Invitation to discuss)

---

Working with the clear intentions used in the examples above, let us now turn them into "I" Statements. If *my intention is to understand what is going on between us so that we can get along better*, I may start the conversation like this:

> I am *worried* [describes feeling] about *how things are going between us* [describes issue], and I would appreciate it if *we could take an afternoon sometime this week to sit down and talk about things* [invitation to discuss].

To choose another illustrative example, if *my intention is to talk about how decisions are made so that I feel more comfortable*, I may start the conversation thus:

> I feel *uncomfortable* [describes feeling] about *our band's decision-making process,* [describes issue] and I would appreciate it if *we could put this topic on the agenda for our next band meeting* [invitation to discuss].

Finally, if *my intention is to express how I feel about how the auditions are going*, I could start the conversation this way:

> I feel *a need to talk* [describes feeling] about *how the auditions are going* [describes issue], and I would appreciate it if we *take the next few minutes and focus on this* [invitation to discuss].

Now in this case, "a need to talk" isn't technically a feeling; it's more of a thought or a judgment (as you'll recall from our previous discussion). It does, however, point directly to a need, i.e., a need to connect, be heard, for fairness, transparency, etc., so we can let it go.

Once you have opened with your "I" Statement, and the other person has agreed to continue the discussion (whether immediately or at a future time), then it's time to move to the fourth and final step, which is following the Fifth House Creative Conversations Model.

## Step Four: Follow the 5-Step Fifth House Creative Conversations Model

Following all five steps of the Fifth House Creative Conversations Model will greatly increase your chances of ensuring that the conversation stays focused, productive, and results in a positive outcome. Continue to stick with the two Guiding Principles of Conflict Resolution throughout the discussion: Avoid the Conflict Escalation Triggers, and always use Active Listening. Never rush through the phases of this model. Take your time—the end result will be worth it. Depending on the situation, you may find that all you need is twenty minutes, or you may need to have a number of different meetings to work through the phases. It all depends on the complexity of the conflict and people's willingness to come to a resolution.

Let's assume you have *assessed the situation* using the diagnostic tools discussed in Part I, and are reasonably certain that this is a situation that doesn't require third party assistance. Let's also assume you have done the following:

1. *Performed your Perception Check* to make sure that there is actually a difficult issue—a conflict—that needs to be addressed with another person or people;

2. *Synchronized your Intention and the desired Impact* to ensure that you are taking next steps for the benefit of all concerned and to genuinely improve the situation; and

3. *Used "I" Statements* to invite a discussion that will lead to resolution of the issue.

Having accomplished these, you are ready for Step #4, i.e., to begin your 5-step Fifth House Creative Conversation.

Note: it is possible that at this stage you aren't sure whether or not to seek outside help. You know there is a problem, you've done the diagnostics, but you still aren't absolutely certain whether help is required, or perhaps you think you need some help but for some reason cannot find/get some. If either one of these conditions exists you could still follow the Fifth House Creative Conversations Model, but build into the discussion your uncertainty about doing this on your own. Be up front about the fact that you'd like to try—or conversely, that you feel uneasy about—resolving the conflict without any third party assistance. Be equally clear that if things don't go well, you will both agree that you will stop and work together to find someone who can assist you in resolving the problem.

Either way, if you've arrived at this point in an actual situation, then you are getting into the heart of conflict resolution. Congratulations! The road ahead may still be bumpy, but regardless of the outcome it will help to remind yourself that what you are about to do—addressing a conflict with another person—is very courageous. You are being real. You are doing the right thing.

It will also help to remind yourself:

- Do your best to stick to all the tips and tools you've learned, such as decoding feelings, needs, and strategies (refer back to Part II, starting on page 59) and engaging consistently in Active Listening (starting on page 105).

- Doing your best does not mean you will be perfect. You might even have a spectacular screw-up. If something goes wrong on your end, you can either just say that it happened—acknowledge it to the other person—and move on, or you can ask to put a hold on the conversation and come back to it later on when you've regrouped. Either option is good.

- Resolving a conflict does not mean that everything will necessarily be rosy between you or will go back to the way it was before the conflict arose. If the conflict is relatively low-level and stays out of the realm of the personal, it will be fairly easy and natural for everyone to just forget about it and get back to normal. However, in other situations the conflict may be more complex, with significant hurt, frustration, or disappointment in play. In such cases, remember that healing between people, and within yourself, does not mean that no damage was ever done. Physical wounds can still leave scars, and so can mental or emotional wounds. It doesn't mean that the incident never happened. It means that anything you have individually and collectively experienced does not govern your relationship— you do. If both of you decide to fix things between you and get on with the beautiful business of making music, then it will be so. Just do your best, and if you need help, get it.

# The Five Steps of a Fifth House Creative Conversations Model

We call this process a *Creative Conversation* because it allows the parties to a conflict the chances to build something fresh, new, and vital from something that might feel stale, old, or unhealthy. We hope that framing it in this way will encourage people to participate, rather than expect such a conversation to be simply another gripe session or the continuation of an argument, fraught with negativity. We also christened it that way because, once completed, such a conversation allows you to get on with the business of being creative.

Throughout the Conversation you will be doing your best to use all of the tips and skills that you have learned from this book so far. It is critical that you go through the steps in sequence and do your best not to deviate from them. Resist the temptation to follow wherever the conversation takes you, for three key reasons:

- First, you are in a tenuous situation and want to ensure a positive outcome. This means you will have to actively shape the course of the conversation to achieve the desired result—leave nothing to chance. Even improvisational jazz follows certain musical rules! In order to maximize your chances of success, strategy is required.

- Second, in order for genuine understanding between the two of you to take place, you are going to have to work at it. Many people are only ready to resolve conflict when they feel understood, but mutual understanding doesn't happen on its own. You are going to have to take the time and effort to get to the place where you

## TIPS FOR OPENING THE CREATIVE CONVERSATIONS DIALOGUE

If you want to make sure the creative conversation goes well, there are a few extra things you can do to set the stage before launching into the dialogue:

- *Set the stage.* Thank the other person for coming to talk, and make sure they are comfortable and ready to start. Confirm that you are both there to try to understand each other and to figure out how to resolve things together. This acknowledges the other person for their willingness to work things out and sets the tone for a meaningful and creative conversation.

- *Check your times.* Confirm how much time you each have to spend on this conversation. This is important because you don't want to run short on time and risk skipping any steps or taking any shortcuts that could undermine your best attempt at patching things up.

both sincerely comprehend each other, in order to resolve matters and move on. Each of the steps in this model is designed to build understanding between you. Each level of understanding is a prerequisite for the next, deeper level of understanding.

- Third, if you don't follow the steps, you may end up fixing things—but they may be the *wrong* things. It's normal for people with the best of intentions to want to proceed straight to solutions, and while solutions are definitely desirable, first make sure that they are aimed at resolving the *real, underlying issues* and not merely their symptoms.

For example, it may seem obvious that the solution to disorganized rehearsal times is to fix a solid schedule. But it could be that the underlying issue is that one or two band members don't feel like they belong, which is the real reason why rehearsal times have been spotty. In a situation like this, scheduled rehearsal times may appear to the untrained eye as a workable solution, but the actual reason *why* rehearsal times were dodgy goes undiscovered. Thus

---

### TIPS FOR OPENING THE CREATIVE CONVERSATIONS DIALOGUE

- *Agree on confidentiality.* Discuss whether or not you want to keep this conversation private between the two of you, and whether or not you are OK with other people knowing about it, under what conditions, etc.

- *Set expectations around behaviours.* Talk about behaviours that you are both OK, and not OK with, e.g., "Even if you don't agree with what I am saying, please try really hard to listen and understand," or, "Let's agree not to interrupt each other."

- *Get commitment.* Agree to do your best to have a really good conversation and fix the problems. Also, agree that if the conversation doesn't work out as well as you would both like, the two of you will either get some help from a third party or try again another time.

the wrong thing is "fixed," and the underlying problem remains.

The Fifth House Creative Conversations Model is a powerful collaborative discussion because it demonstrates to everyone concerned that their perspectives are being taken seriously, and that as human beings they are important. Initiating a collaborative discussion with someone you are in conflict with shows that you care about them and the situation, and that your intention is to arrive at a resolution that works for everyone. This will be received as a signal of respect and will create a safe atmosphere in which to discuss difficult issues. If you want the other person to get on board and roll up their sleeves to resolve things together with you, *this* is how they must experience you!

Naturally you want to resolve issues and get back to normal as quickly as possible. These desires and intentions are another positive sign. However, navigating through conflict and emotions can be tricky, and moving too quickly from problem to solution is seldom a good idea. Taking your time and doing things right will put everyone in the best frame of mind to use their extraordinary creativity to find lasting solutions and resolve matters for the longer term.

Follow the steps of this Model, and may healing magic unfold!

The 5 Steps of the Fifth House Creative Conversations Model are as follows:

1. Tell each other your stories.
2. Identify what you want to resolve.
3. Develop options and potential solutions.
4. Articulate agreement and set follow-up meeting.
5. Hold follow-up meeting to ensure everything is working.

Let's analyze each stage of the Model. If you follow along, you will notice that we have given you some "to do" tips for each of the stages. Generally speaking, if you are using the skills and keeping in mind the Guiding Principles while following each of these five steps, you will be conducting a *bona fide* conflict resolution session. Visit the Resources section our website for an example of a Fifth House Creative Conversations dialogue illustrating each of the stages of the model and containing pointers for each. Have a look at the theory below, and then watch/listen to it come to life with the example afterward.

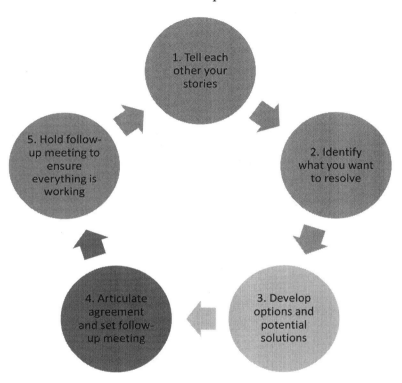

1. **Tell each other your stories:**

   a. *Describe the problem or situation you have come to talk about.* The primary thing to remember here is that you stay very far away from using the Conflict Escalation Triggers as described on page 92. Use neutral, non-accusatory words and tone. Avoid blame or judgments. Don't exaggerate. The best way is to start with an "I Statement" (e.g., "I felt _____ when I noticed that _____was happening, and my goal in having this meeting is to _____" as per the three-part "I statement" model recommended on page 134).

b.  *Invite the other person to speak about the problem or situation from his/her perspective.* Listen to understand by using Active Listening skills (see page 105) and by staying genuinely curious about the other person's perspective.

c.  *When the other person has finished describing the situation from their perspective, and you have demonstrated that you have understood what they have said (see page 116), it is then your turn to describe the situation from your perspective.* It is tough to do, but make it your goal to understand the other person first—before you try to get them to understand you. Quite simply, if they feel heard, understood, and taken seriously, they are far more likely to be willing and able to make the effort to hear, understand, and take you seriously. Do for them first, what you would like them to do for you.

2.  **Identify what you want to resolve:**

a.  *Have an honest and open discussion about what is important to each of you.* Take as much time as you need, because everything else from here on out hinges on this. When the time comes to find solutions, you will want to make sure you are fixing the right things—and you can only do that if you get this part right. Stay focused on *what* needs to be fixed, not who. Stay away from taking a position or going straight to solutions (you'll develop solutions collaboratively, in due course). Talk about what your concerns are; as you are each doing so, help each other to articulate what is underlying these concerns. Explore the needs that are at stake for each of you. Get clear about what "this" is all really about, for each of you. Write these things down. Again, take as much time as you need. Don't rush it—get it right.

b.  *Make a list of the things that need to be fixed and/or issues that need to be resolved.* From all of the above (a), make a list of the issues that each of you have identified as being important. If there are several, agree on a starting point and the order or sequence for addressing each of them in turn. There is no "right" or "wrong" order; you might want to tackle the most contentious issue(s) first, or conversely, build up to that point with the smaller, less contentious issue(s).

c. *Ask if there is anything else that is important to him or her that s/he might want to share.* Check to make sure nothing has been left unsaid. It is possible that someone may still have something to express that, for whatever reason, they haven't felt comfortable bringing up yet. If there is something else that comes up, repeat (a) and (b) above.

**3. Develop options and potential solutions:**

a. Together, *brainstorm creative ways of resolving the issues and taking care of what is important to you.* We call these options because they're all possible solutions, or parts of the solution, to the problem at hand. They should remain potential solutions for most of this stage; avoid the temptation to leap straight to declaring the most obvious, quickest or easiest answer. Let all the ideas marinate.

It's best to do the brainstorming while sitting side-by-side and recording ideas on paper or on a white board, flip chart, or other medium. This symbolically demonstrates a joint effort in solving the problem and reinforces the idea at a subtle psychological level. Talking across a table places a physical and psychological barrier between you and puts you in literal opposition to each other.

As you proceed, follow these key brainstorming principles:

- Initially, the *quantity* of ideas is more important than the *quality.* You will go back later and either develop or filter out the less viable ones. The more ideas you have to work with, the better.

- All ideas or fragments of ideas, however tentative, should be noted without judgment, comment, or committing to any particular idea or proposed solution. This means no censoring or shooting down the other's ideas and no self-censoring, either.

The goal of this step is to remain open to all creative input, no matter how outlandish or unworkable the ideas may seem at first. Proper brainstorming encourages the rapid, open flow of creativity, and it lessens the likelihood that someone's feelings will be hurt by editorializing on those ideas as they emerge. You never know which idea will provide the platform for the best, most durable solution, or who will contribute it. The more all parties can contribute to the solution(s), the more likely everyone will be able to throw their wholehearted support behind it/them.

   b. *Identify the potential solution(s) by agreeing on the most promising ideas and developing them further.* The ideal solution seldom exists "in the wild" and usually needs some modification to make it more viable or appealing to one or more of the parties. An idea may be unworkable in its present form, but, with a little tweaking, an otherwise unlikely solution may come to life. For example, let's say a group is brainstorming ways to resolve rehearsal scheduling conflicts but the schedules simply don't mesh and it's simply not realistic to ask one band member to quit his or her job to make it work. One possible solution is to hold asynchronous rehearsals, i.e., at different times for different members until you can all be together at the same time. On its surface, this idea seems ludicrous, but, considering all the inexpensive home studio technology currently available, it may be possible for most of the group to record their rehearsals "live," while the other member(s) practices by playing along at home and recording the results. While it may not be the ideal solution, and it may not be chosen in the end, but it certainly is a lot more feasible than everyone rehearsing live at different times or trying to make otherwise irreconcilable schedules overlap.

Of course eventually identifying the "right" or "best" solution can be a challenge. One way to ensure that the solution chosen is at least fair to all parties—and not just "fair" to one because it works out better for them—is to *establish objective criteria for choosing the solution*. For example, if you were in disagreement over the value of a damaged second-hand instrument, you could use eBay's average asking price for that same make and model as one criterion for determining what is fair to both the person who damaged the instrument and the person who owned it. Otherwise, setting an arbitrary value risks favouring one party over the other, and by definition the solution will not be fair to both parties. In the previous example, a fair solution might require that no member of the band has to quit their job to make the schedule work. Remember, too, that the best solution may in fact be a combination of ideas, either in their original form or in some modified version.

Only once the brainstorming is truly finished, and all ideas are completely exhausted, is it time to go through each and every solution listed and weigh them against each person's interests, needs, and any objective decision-making criteria you have set. Avoid rushing to judgment at all costs. Brainstorming is a wonderful opportunity to use your creativity!

4. **Articulate Agreement and set follow-up meeting:**

   a. *Agree on the most appropriate solution(s).* The "most appropriate" solutions are those that realistically address the greatest number of concerns and needs of all parties and achieve a truly "win-win" outcome. If you've followed all the steps to this point and have had a sufficiently productive, open-minded brainstorming session then chances are you'll have no trouble identifying the most workable resolution.

   b. *Clearly articulate the terms of the agreement*—for example, who does what, when, where, and how. Be very specific and ensure that you are both clear on your roles and responsibilities and that everyone else is equally clear on theirs. Nothing will undo a satisfying agreement (and lead right back into conflict) more predictably than having someone fail to uphold their end of the deal, and one way to ensure they keep their word is to simply make sure they know what's expected of them. Never assume everyone automatically understands or remembers what's been agreed.

c.  *Develop a contingency plan to address what you will do if things don't go as planned.* While this collaborative discussion model is relatively foolproof, things can sometimes go sideways. It's always a good idea to have a "Plan B," even at the best of times, so you can have one to fall back on in the event your original win-win solution doesn't stand the test of time.

d.  *Revisit confidentiality to be clear on what can and cannot be shared with others.* You might, for example, decide that it's OK for everyone to share with their significant others how the experience impacted them emotionally, but not who said or did what. Conversely, you might collectively decide that nothing about the situation should ever be discussed outside the rehearsal studio. Whatever provides the most peace of mind and feeling of safety/security for all parties is the right approach.

e.  *Write all of this (A to D) down!* You should each keep a copy of what has been decided and recorded. This is a simple way of preventing any potential problems because someone has forgotten exactly what was agreed upon, or details got missed or mixed up, etc.; you can always refer back to the written notes as needed. In fact, it might be a good idea to make a habit of periodically checking in to see how you are doing with the agreement, even if things seem to be going well between you. If someone is starting to feel things slip, then it's a good opportunity to reaffirm the agreement and recommit to upholding it. If everything is indeed fine, then you can feel positive about the strength and solidity of your agreement.

f. *Close the conversation.* Thank the other party for agreeing to work with you to resolve the situation. This brings a sense of closure to the incident and rewards everyone for their patience and hard work.

g. *Set a date & time for a follow-up meeting.* This is critical. The reasons for this are explained in Step #5 below.

h. *Give yourselves a huge pat on the back!* You've earned it.

**5. Hold follow-up meeting to ensure everything is working:**

It's dangerous to assume that everything will go as planned. People are people, they fall back into familiar, comfortable routines, things get forgotten, and before you know it there's another upset. If you follow up diligently to make sure everyone stays on track, there's a greater likelihood that the decisions made at the problem-solving Creative Conversation will stick. Revisit the agreement(s) periodically to make sure it's still working; there's no law saying that a solution that isn't working to everyone's benefit can't be changed.

Perhaps most importantly, make sure that everyone looks out for each other. It's easy (and natural) for everyone to take care to protect their own feelings and needs, but it can't come at the expense of someone else's.

## Summary

In this section we identified and learned to apply two Guiding Principles of conflict prevention and resolution: avoiding the common Conflict Escalation Triggers and using Active Listening techniques. Triggers include using the word "you" in any conversation related to a conflict, because the other party will inevitably mistake it for an accusation of some sort. Often the words that follow "you" attribute their behaviour to bad intent, carelessness, or some other reason that is likely to be as incorrect as it is shameful; this begins a cycle of blame and retribution. Other Triggers include dredging up old or irrelevant issues and attempting to "triangulate" by getting others in your corner, usually by telling tales that cast you as the hero or victim of the story and the other party as the bad guy.

Another way to ensure your conflict resolution conversations don't go sideways is to use a checklist to ensure you follow all four steps to conflict resolution, i.e., first doing a Perception Check, synchronizing the intent and the impact of the conversation, using "I" Statements, and following the 5-step Fifth House Creative Conversations Model. The first of these steps is simply a way to verify whether there's actually a problem to begin with, or if it's someone's mistaken perception that is causing the apparent issue. This often eliminates the need for any subsequent work. If it doesn't, the second step is a way to ensure that any negative impact of the conversation and its content—which might cause pain or discomfort for one or more of the people involved—is clearly unintentional. The real purpose of the conversation (and this second step) is not to make anyone feel bad or wrong but to ensure the intentions behind the parties' words and deeds (which are often good and noble) have the desired emotional effect (which can otherwise turn out negative and hurtful).

Once this foundation is established, keep the lines of communication open by ensuring you speak only from your own feelings and experience, thus precluding the possibility that you might accidentally blame or accuse the other person. Along with speaking from your own feelings and experience in "I" Statements, use Active Listening (paraphrasing, summarizing, and practising empathy); restating and reframing the other's words will give them the opportunity to correct any mistaken impressions, and reassure them they've truly been heard. Finally, following each of the five steps in the Fifth House Creative Conversations Model (especially if you prepare well using the checklists and worksheets provided) will help ensure a positive outcome for all involved.

# Conclusion

By now you have probably learned far more than you ever thought you would learn—or might need to learn—about resolving conflicts successfully. You might have approached this book (or at least the topic of conflict) full of dread. Our hope is that if we define conflict as a signal that something, somewhere, needs to change, it gives cause for optimism in the sense that you can empower yourself with the tools to make the necessary adjustments.

We began by looking at the history of conflict in the music industry, which is long, dramatic, and has left a trail of economic and artistic destruction. It's sad to think of the great recordings never made, the tours cut short, and the careers effectively ruined, all because of needless conflicts. Think of the creative output had they been managed well, instead. That's the bad news.

The good news is that you are now armed with some basic conflict theory (from Part I) to illustrate just how costly conflict can be, and why. Much of that cost remains hidden, but it manifests in a wide array of problems, from absenteeism, to physical illness, to significant financial loss.

Having read this book, you now know the difference between mere disagreement, conflict, and harassment or bullying, which is an important distinction, because it gives you a better idea of how to handle each, and it lets you know when things have progressed to an undesirable stage. Likewise, you also know how to recognize the four warning signs of conflict (emotional, physical, behavioural, and relational) so that you can stop a conflict in its tracks before it has a chance to devolve into a worse situation.

You now have sufficient knowledge to not only assess a conflict situation on the basis of emotions, trust, history, and power dynamics, but also determine when it's time to get help managing or resolving a conflict. There are several types of conflict resolution assistance available, and you can decide which is (are) more appropriate to a particular level of conflict and where to locate resources for assistance with conflict resolution. Even if you still don't feel confident in your own conflict resolution abilities, you can relax in the knowledge that some form of expert help is at hand regardless of your current skill level.

By now you have analyzed the inner mechanics of conflict and examined the critical role that feelings play in conflict situations. You have learned how to interpret feelings that may arise in conflict situations, and you can then use that information to help parse your own needs and better understand the needs of the other party—even if they're having trouble identifying and understanding their own feelings. *Needs*, whether we fully comprehend them or not, are central to conflict resolution; if we know that another musician craves acknowledgement for their contributions (for example), it allows us to meet those needs without necessarily having to sacrifice our own. All we have to do is remember to offer acknowledgements like, "Hey, I really like that riff,"—even if it doesn't work in the context of the song you're writing at that moment. You might be able to use the part somewhere else, and in the meantime you've helped keep your fellow musician happier than if you had just dismissed it outright.

In Part II, the term *strategies* was defined (in the context of conflict situations) as attempts to meet those needs, however clumsy or unintentionally hurtful they may be. We resort to these reactionary, primitive strategies when we haven't got the words or tools to express our needs more effectively—often because we're in the midst of an emotional storm. Being able to interpret strategies as such allows you to get underneath the turmoil and look past the otherwise incomprehensible behaviours to figure out what you might need to say or do in order to meet the other person's needs and, hopefully, avoid or de-escalate conflict.

Another skill you learned in Part II is how to differentiate authentic feelings from blaming feelings. This, too, is critical, because when someone's ability to articulate their feelings drops (including our own), you can do two things: first, prevent yourself being triggered by someone else's blaming feeling statements, and second, interpret the situation correctly and avoid fanning the flames.

In Part III you delved deeper into essential conflict prevention and resolution skills, including the application of two Guiding Principles: avoiding the common Conflict Escalation Triggers and listening actively. You learned how to use a checklist to ensure you follow all four steps to conflict resolution (conducting a Perception Check, synchronizing your intent and desired impact, speaking only in "I" statements, and following the Fifth House Creative Conversations Model, step-by-step).

Congratulations! We hope you've been able to follow along and perhaps even apply some of your newfound skills to a situation you might be facing right now in your group or personal life. In getting this far you have joined a select (but, fortunately, growing) community of immensely talented, creative people who have the necessary skills, attitudes, and knowledge to prevent conflicts from occurring in the first place. If conflicts do occur, as is sometimes inevitable, your expertise will reduce the likelihood of their escalating out of control and help to resolve them effectively. Practice your conflict resolution skills, because, like anything else worth learning, they require patience and commitment to develop. We wish you every success in your musical career, and may you spread joy and harmony everywhere you go, not only with your music but with your life skills, too.

May all your conflicts be resolved quietly and all your music be played loud!

# Acknowledgements

*Helene*: My parents, Alain and Marianne, were a profound influence on me in that they agreed at the very start of their marriage that they would never have an argument in front of their children. They held steadfastly true to this agreement without ever wavering once. My brother and sister and I reaped the benefit of this all of our lives. I have my parents to thank for this inspiration, which led me to a lifelong career as a practitioner and educator of conflict resolution.

To all those confused and hurting young people that I worked with as a criminal and young offender mediator; to all those families and children torn apart by separation and divorce when I worked as a family mediator; and to all those stressed-out individuals and groups I worked with as a workplace conflict resolution consultant: thank you for allowing me to enter onto the sacred ground of your vulnerabilities and pain. Each time, I honed my skills just a little bit more. Each time, I understood just a little bit more about the human condition. Each time, I saw my own reflection in the mirrors of your situations, and learned. All along, my clients, colleagues, and students have been my greatest teachers. I am immensely grateful to all of you.

My daughter Emme, upon hearing that I was going to write this book, immediately went out and bought me my first laptop with her own hard-earned money. I will never forget this unhesitating show of confidence and support. All three of my children have been cheering me on throughout this process—my love for them knows no bounds. Also, special thanks to our family friend Patrick Shanahan, for his feedback on earlier drafts.

Finally, to my co-author Ken Ashdown, goes my deepest thanks and respect. Never, in our high school days, would I ever have thought we would one day write a book together. Ah, but such is the beauty and magic of life.

*Ken*: Throughout my career I have had the great fortune of working with countless extremely smart and talented people, and I have been equally blessed writing this book. I must thank my co-author, Helene, for suggesting the collaboration in the first place and having the vision and perseverance to finally pursue it with me so many years later. My wife Danika is not only the love of my life and a tremendous inspiration but also a successful author, screenwriter, poet, and editor whose input was invaluable; thanks for your ongoing support and encouragement. Jennifer D. Munro was not only lightning-fast but also deadly accurate and judicious with her editor's pen. Thanks to Jeff Blancato for the proofreading assistance. To paraphrase the meme: "All our mistakes are belong to us." Tod McCoy of Hydra House Press was an invaluable ally and a source of much-needed e-publishing expertise. I am grateful to my thousands of clients and students, past and present, for gifting me with your presence and for allowing me the honour of serving you. Last but not least, this book would not have been possible without the ongoing support and friendship of the Men's Team: thank you Dean, Les, David, Leonard, Dieter, and Dan.

# Appendix: Worksheets and Checklists

The worksheets in this section are meant to help you prepare for handling a difficult situation on your own. There are four in all:

1. Conflict Assessment Worksheet (to help evaluate the emotions, trust, history and power dynamic in a conflict)

2. Conflict Assistance Chart (to help you determine what kind of assistance, if any, is most appropriate for your situation)

3. Preparation Checklist (to help ensure you are ready to follow all four steps of the Conflict Resolution)

4. Fifth House Creative Conversations Preparation Worksheet (to help you prepare for the 5-step Fifth House Creative Conversation to follow).

You can also download and print PDF versions from the Fifth House Group website (www.fifthhousegroup.com/CRFMworksheets.html) any time you find yourself needing to prepare for a potentially challenging or uncomfortable conversation; where applicable, completed examples are also available to show you how to make best use of them.

Before attempting to resolve a conflict on your own, make sure you can put a check mark in every box on the Preparation Checklist! When things get emotional, it's far too easy to accidentally say or do something that winds up causing further distress unless you've really done your best to have a genuinely collaborative problem-solving discussion. Use the many other resources at your disposal on the Fifth House Group web site, and good luck!

# Conflict Assessment Worksheet

| Criteria | Score | | | | |
|---|---|---|---|---|---|
| **Emotions** (1 = Low levels of emotion; 5 = intense or high levels) | 1 | 2 | 3 | 4 | 5 |
| **Trust** (1 = Good, strong trust between people; 5 = Poor or no trust) | 1 | 2 | 3 | 4 | 5 |
| **History** (1 = Little or no history of conflict; 5 = long or substantial history of conflict) | 1 | 2 | 3 | 4 | 5 |
| **Power** (1 = Equality of power/ fair & balanced; 5 = great imbalance/high inequality) | 1 | 2 | 3 | 4 | 5 |
| **Total score:** | | | | | |

**Interpretation:** A score of **4-6** indicates you can probably safely handle this situation on your own; **7-13** indicates you should probably seek some third party assistance; **14-20** indicates you should probably not attempt to resolve the conflict without some professional intervention.

**Notes, observations, and conclusion:**

# Conflict Assistance Chart

**Note**: Use the previous *Conflict Assessment Worksheet* to evaluate the relative levels of emotion, trust, history, and any power imbalance in the conflict.

| Factor: | Coaching | Negotiation | Facilitation | Mediation |
|---|---|---|---|---|
| **Emotions** | Any | Low to Medium | Medium | High |
| **Trust Levels** | Any | Good to Medium | Medium | Low |
| **History** | Any | None or Positive | Some | Some or Negative |
| **Power Imbalance** | Any | None or Some | Some | Yes |

# Preparation Checklist

| Preparation Checklist | |
|---|---|
| **Item** | **Check ✓** |
| **Description of conflict:** *I have assessed and described the conflict in terms of the Emotions, Trust, History, and Power dynamic, and it is appropriate for us to handle this without a third party.* | |
| **Triggers to watch out for:** *I have learned the common Conflict Escalation Triggers and avoided using them. I have noticed when others use them and avoided getting triggered myself.* | |
| **Ways To Demonstrate I am Listening:** *I have used some or all of the Active Listening techniques to show the other party(ies) that I am listening.* | |
| **Perception Check:** *I have checked my perceptions and tested them to see if they correspond to reality.* | |
| **Intent vs. Impact:** *I have synchronized the intent (motive or purpose) of the conversation and of any statements made to ensure the proper emotional impact.* | |
| **Opening "I" Statement:** *I have prepared an opening statement framed as something about me and my feelings or needs, rather than about him/her.* | |
| **Fifth House Creative Conversation discussion points:** *I have developed a list of discussion points that give us a helpful, mutually agreeable starting point for our problem-solving.* | |

If you really want to increase your chances of having a successful conversation, the next worksheet is also well worth the time it takes to complete. Once again, like the other worksheets presented here, the Fifth House Creative Conversations Preparation Worksheet is available as a free download from the Fifth House Group website.

# Fifth House Creative Conversations Preparation Worksheet

1. **Gather the information:**

   What are your observations of the situation? What was said or done, and what were the circumstances? Stick to the actual words and actions heard & seen, and avoid making assumptions or attributing behaviours or causes. Note only the things that any neutral observer would agree to be true. (**Note:** use extra pages where required.)

2. **Pause for self-reflection** (be completely honest when describing the following):

   - What's important to me: What need is being threatened or challenged here? What is it about this situation that is getting me anxious?
   - My attitude: Am I entrenched in a position or being unnecessarily aggressive? Is this really about me being right and the other person being wrong? Am I truly interested in solving the problem together, or am I looking to score points? Am I avoiding the situation, hoping it will go away or get better on its own?
   - My hot buttons: What are the things that trigger me? What words or actions readily cause me to feel insulted, defensive, or angry?
   - My emotions and how I might react: What do I need to do to make sure I don't get destructive?
   - Does anyone else need to be involved in this conversation before decisions are made?

3. **Pause to reflect on the other person:**
   - What's important to him/her?
   - His/her attitude: What can I do to make sure s/he feels as safe and comfortable as possible?
   - His/her hot buttons: What are they? What can I do to make sure I don't pull any Conflict Escalation Triggers?
   - His/her emotions: How might they react? What can I do to make sure I don't contribute to a negative reaction?

4. **Next steps:**
   - Review the Preparation Checklist.
   - Prepare to raise the issue and extend an invitation to the other person.
   - Prepare and suggest a date/time and the duration of meeting.
   - Determine the location (consider physical layout, comfort, discretion, neutrality, no distractions).

5. **Review the 5-step Fifth House Creative Conversations Model:**

   a. Tell each other your stories.

   b. Identify what you want to resolve.

   c. Develop Options and potential solutions.

   d. Articulate Agreement and set follow-up meeting.

   e. Hold follow-up meeting to ensure everything is working.

# About the Authors

**Helene Arts**, CEO of Fifth House Group, started off thinking that she was going to become a lawyer, but by 1995 she realized that the gods had other plans for her and thus began her career as a professional mediator. Since then she has been a full time consultant in the field of conflict resolution within criminal, family, and civil court systems, and in not-for-profit and corporate workplace settings. Along the way she became fascinated with group dynamics, and in 2004 completed a Masters in Human Systems Intervention at Concordia University in Montreal, Quebec, becoming a specialist in group intervention. For over ten years Helene has also taught university courses in subjects such as mediation, interpersonal communication, group dynamics, conflict resolution, organizational conflict, and group facilitation. She holds a special place in her heart for creative people of all kinds.

Fifth House Group President **Ken Ashdown** is a musician and former music journalist, indie label entrepreneur, and major label executive. Over his career Ken has worked with some of the music industry's biggest stars, including Shania Twain, Def Leppard, Bon Jovi, John Mellencamp, Dire Straits, New Order, David Bowie, the Pixies, and U2. He served as Vice President at PolyGram Group Canada (Mercury/Polydor division) and later at QDesign Corporation, a leading provider of advanced digital audio compression technologies. An award-winning, certified adult educator, Ken spent several years as Head of Department at Vancouver Film School's innovative Entertainment Business Management transmedia program and has been described as a "master teacher." He earned his Master of Arts (MA) degree in Music Business Management (with Distinction) from the University of Westminster in London, England. In addition to curating the back catalogue for his independent publishing company and record label, his greatest passions include leadership, environmental issues, and sustainability.

# Index

# T

# V

# W

Made in the USA
Lexington, KY
03 April 2015